INTERNATIONAL PUBLIC GOODS

INTERNATIONAL PUBLIC GOODS

*Incentives, Measurement,
and Financing*

Edited by
Marco Ferroni and Ashoka Mody

KLUWER ACADEMIC PUBLISHERS
Boston / Dordrecht / London

THE WORLD BANK
Washington, DC

Distributors for North, Central and South America:
Kluwer Academic Publishers
101 Philip Drive
Assinippi Park
Norwell, Massachusetts 02061 USA
Telephone (781) 871-6600
Fax (781) 871-6528
E-Mail < kluwer@wkap.com>

Distributors for all other countries:
Kluwer Academic Publishers Group
Distribution Centre
Post Office Box 322
3300 AH Dordrecht, THE NETHERLANDS
Telephone 31 78 6392 392
Fax 31 78 6546 474
  E-Mail < services@wkap.nl>

   Electronic Services < http://www.wkap.nl>

Library of Congress Cataloging-in-Publication Data

A C.I.P. Catalogue record for this book is available from the Library of Congress

ISBN: 0-4020-7144-4 (hbk)
ISBN: 0-8213-5110-9 (pbk)

CONTENTS

PREFACE AND ACKNOWLEDGMENTS

Many development problems transcend national borders and are regional, or even global, in character. The recognition of these international challenges, which range from the transmission of disease across borders to the spread of global financial instability, has led to a new urgency to contain and resolve them. Because no one country acting on its own can typically deal with such challenges, international coordination is required, but is typically difficult to achieve. The World Bank's *Global Development Finance 2001: Building Coalitions for Effective Development Finance,* published in April 2001, discusses this evolving concern. That report offers a strategic and operational framework for supplying international public goods and mobilizing the required financial resources. The report also presents a first set of estimates on the extent of international resource transfers for these goods. A number of papers were written as background to the report. The purpose of this book is to briefly present the principal conclusions from *Global Development Finance 2001,* but mainly to make the background papers available to an academic and policy audience. We expect that the analytical and empirical contributions of this research would be of wide interest.

This books marks the completion of a process initiated by a workshop on Global Public Policies and Program held on July 11–12, 2000, in Washington, D.C. to outline the analytical and strategic agenda for the delivery of international public goods. Several leading academics and senior policymakers joined in the deliberations at the workshop, organized jointly by the United Nations Development Programme and the World Bank. For making that workshop possible and for the publication of its proceedings, the authors are grateful to Christopher Gerard and Robert Picciotto of the World Bank's Operations Evaluation Department. Throughout, the Swiss Agency for Development and Cooperation provided financial support. The editors and authors are grateful to the agency, and especially to Walter Hofer, for the support and encouragement offered. However, the views expressed in the book are those of the authors and not necessarily those of the World Bank or the Swiss Agency for Development and Cooperation.

The editors are also grateful to many who have graciously shared their ideas and their time in reviewing various drafts. Nancy Birdsall, Ravi Kanbur, and Bruce Ross-Larson were with us throughout the project. Robert Devlin, Ishac Diwan, Nagy Hanna, Paul Hubbard, Gregory Ingram, Paul Isenman, Motoo Kusakabe, Geoffrey Lamb, Uma Lele, and Stephen Quick helped at different stages. We would especially like to acknowledge the contribution of Aristomene Varoudakis, who was our coauthor for the *Global Development Finance* report. Finally, we would like to thank Alice Faintich for her excellent editing and attention to detail, Kathy Rettinger for proofreading the manuscript, and Cindy Stock for typesetting it.

CONTRIBUTORS

Scott Barrett

Scott Barrett is professor of environmental economics and international political economy at the Paul H. Nitze School of Advanced International Studies, Johns Hopkins University. He previously taught at the London Business School. Professor Barrett has written a number of papers on international cooperation and treaty negotiation, especially in the area of the environment, for which he was awarded the Erik Kempe prize. He received a Ph.D. in economics from the London School of Economics. He can be reached at sbarrett@jhu.edu.

Marco Ferroni

Throughout his career in international development, Marco Ferroni has held posts in multilateral and bilateral agencies. He recently joined the Office of Evaluation and Oversight of the Inter-American Development Bank. Immediately prior to this, he was senior advisor in the World Bank's Vice Presidency for Resource Mobilization and Cofinancing. Dr. Ferroni has been a member of the boards of executive directors of the Inter-American Development Bank and the Inter-American Investment Corporation, and has occupied managerial positions in the Swiss ministries of Public Economy and Foreign Affairs, working in the area of technical and financial cooperation with developing countries and emerging market economies. He held a graduate teaching appointment at the Swiss Federal Institute of Technology in Zurich in the 1990s. Dr. Ferroni has published articles and professional papers on foreign aid and development finance, international public goods, public expenditure reform, policy reform and social protection, and the inter-relationship between trade and macroeconomic regimes and agricultural growth. He received a Ph.D. in agricultural economics from Cornell University. He can be reached at marcof@iadb.org.

Adrian Hewitt

Adrian Hewitt was one of the original associates of Robert Cassen on *Does Aid Work?* (Oxford University Press, Oxford, U.K., 1984, revised 1994) and wrote *Crisis or Transition in Foreign Aid* (Overseas Development Institute [ODI], London, 1994, with the Overseas Development Council, Washington, D.C., and the North-South Institute, Ottawa). In 1984 he founded the All-Party Parliamentary Group on Overseas Development in the British House of Commons, with which he wrote *Africa's Multilateral Debt: A Modest Proposal* (ODI, London, 1994), a tract that preceded the agitation for and the realization of the present heavily indebted poor countries arrangements. Educated at Oxford University and the School of Oriental and African Studies, London, he worked in Madagascar and Malawi before joining the ODI in London, where he is now senior research fellow and director of the ODI Fellowship Scheme. Mr. Hewitt is co-editor of *Development Policy Review* and a board member of *Third World Quarterly* and the Paris-based economics research institute DIAL. Recent publications include *Economic Crisis in Developing Countries: New Perspectives on Commodities, Trade and Finance* (with Machiko Nissanke, Pinter Publishers, London, 1993), *Europe's Preferred Partners: The Lomé Countries in World Trade* (with Michael Davenport, ODI, London, 1995), and *World Commodity Prices: Still a Problem for Developing Countries?* (with Sheila Page, ODI, London, 2001). He can be reached at a.hewitt@odi.org.uk.

Ashoka Mody

Ashoka Mody is a division chief in the International Monetary Fund's Research Department. Most recently he was at the World Bank, where he was manager and principal author of the Bank's *Global Development Finance 2001*. He has previously worked at AT&T's Bell Laboratories and been a visiting professor of public policy and management at the University of Pennsylvania's Wharton School. He has written on technical change through foreign direct investment and international trade, and more recently on international financial markets and capital flows to developing countries. His writings have been published in academic journals and for policy audiences. He can be reached at amody@imf.org.

Oliver Morrissey

Oliver Morrissey is director of the Centre for Research in Economic Development and International Trade and reader in development economics at the School of Economics, University of Nottingham, where he has been since 1989. He is also a research fellow in international economics with the Overseas Development Institute in London, and has considerable experience in aid and trade policy analysis, working mostly in East Africa. He has published numerous articles in academic journals, notably on aid effectiveness, trade policy reform, and structural adjustment, but also on public choice aspects of public finance. He obtained his Ph.D. in economics from the University of Bath, United Kingdom. He can be reached at Oliver.Morrissey@nottingham.ac.uk.

Todd Sandler

Todd Sandler is the Robert R. and Katheryn A. Dockson Chair of International Relations and Economics at the University of Southern California, Los Angeles. He was previously Distinguished Professor of Economics and Political Science at Iowa State University. His writings address such topics as public goods and externalities, defense and peace economics, environmental economics, and foreign assistance. He authored *Economic Concepts for the Social Sciences* (Cambridge University Press, Cambridge, U.K., forthcoming), *Global Challenges: An Approach to Environmental, Political, and Economic Problems* (Cambridge University Press, Cambridge, U.K., 1997), and *Collective Action: Theory and Applications* (University of Michigan Press, Ann Arbor, 1992). He co-authored *The Theory of Externalities, Public Goods, and Club Goods* (Cambridge University Press, Cambridge, U.K, 2nd edition, 1996). Professor Sandler has worked for numerous organizations, including the United Nations Development Programme, the Overseas Development Council, the U.S. Department of Defense, and the World Bank. In 1998–2000 he was a NATO Fellow. He can be reached at tsandler@usc.edu.

Dirk Willem te Velde

Dirk Willem te Velde is a research fellow at the Overseas Development Institute, where his main interests concern international public goods and the impact of and policies toward foreign direct investment. He was previously a research officer at the National Institute of Economic and Social Research and a researcher based at the CPB Netherlands Bureau for Economic Policy Analysis. He has published a number of articles and book chapters on foreign direct investment, trade, development, labor markets. and the environment. He can be reached at dw.tevelde@odi.org.uk.

Chapter 1

GLOBAL INCENTIVES FOR INTERNATIONAL PUBLIC GOODS:

Introduction and Overview

Marco Ferroni and Ashoka Mody

As the world becomes more integrated through trade, financial flows, and the movement of people, a new set of public policy challenges arises.[1] National policy initiatives are necessary, but insufficient. Indeed, actions taken in the national interest can sometimes make matters worse from an international perspective. Globally coordinated efforts are needed to deal with such challenges as climate change, the AIDS epidemic, and financial crises. If these threats to global stability can induce global incentives to work collectively and cooperatively, they can be turned into opportunities. Humane and equitable globalization requires a shared vision of global prosperity. This shared vision makes possible international public goods (IPGs), which include the *rules* that apply across borders, the *institutions* that supervise and enforce these rules, and the *benefits* that accrue without distinctions between countries. The benefits accrue, for example, in the form of a cleaner environment, the lowered prevalence of disease, a more stable global financial system, and a reduced level of international conflict.

In a wide variety of circumstances, when countries act in their own self-interest, they also contribute to the provision of IPGs. Safe domestic financial systems, better public health, more research and development, and reduced emissions of greenhouse gases are all beneficial from both a domestic and international point of view. For this reason, the supply of IPGs will largely continue to depend on governments' willingness and ability to devote national resources to those domestic objectives that also contribute to international purposes and goals (see Cooper 2001; Kaul 2001).

This book, however, focuses on actions in the international arena that can help complement domestic efforts. The demand for IPGs has grown apace with globalization (see Kaul, Grunberg, and Stern 1999; Sandler 1997). Ferroni (chapter 6 in this volume) infers this growth in demand from the proliferation of regional trading arrangements that, he argues, reflects the need for more effective international rules. Soros (forthcoming), in reflecting on the promise and pitfalls of globalization, also maintains that currently public goods are undersupplied relative to private goods. He recommends more public resources: an amount equivalent to US$30 billion to be reserved annually to finance IPGs, of which more than US$5 billion a year could be spent on dealing with the AIDS epidemic (see also Sachs 2001).

Economic theory supports these assertions. The supply of public goods remains restricted, sometimes severely so, because households, businesses, and governments, acting in isolation, typically do not take into consideration the implications of their actions on others. This makes it difficult to put in place coordinating mechanisms—based on market or other prices—to pay for shared benefits. Markets do not have the ability to allocate sufficient resources to public goods, because private returns typically do not justify the investment in public goods. Further complicating matters, especially when public goods are viewed in an international context, people in different countries may value these shared benefits quite differently. At the same time, with the growing complexity of global interactions, the existing institutional framework is unable to consistently enforce beneficial action when markets prove insufficient.

Thus IPGs pose a policy challenge, because neither markets nor the existing constellation of institutions can effectively and consistently provide the cross-border rules or resources required. Hence the call for greater coordination that brings together official institutions with nongovernmental coalitions and other private parties. However, underlying the widespread agreement on the need for international coordination, two policy questions arise. The first overarching question refers to the institutions that could govern activities with cross-border consequences. In the absence of a global government, various alternatives are possible (Kindleberger 1986). At one extreme, a leader nation can set the agenda and back it up with resources, acting either in its own interests or motivated by broader global objectives. At the other extreme, informal, privately motivated coalitions can act in their areas of advocacy to promote the cause of coordination. In between these extremes, various intergovernmental agreements and official financing mechanisms can serve the coordination function.

The second, more specific, question arises in the context of these official arrangements. What, in particular, is the role of international financial institutions in promoting and financing IPGs? With demand for IPGs strong and rising and supply not following automatically, international organizations have been called on to step up their role, especially with respect to global and regional programs directed toward systemic stability and poverty alleviation (see, for example, International Financial Institutions Advisory Commission 2000; Kanbur, Sandler, and Morrison 1999; Kaul, Grunberg, and Stern 1999; Sachs 2000; Summers 2000). Thus international organizations are being pushed beyond their traditional country programs to tackle both regional and global cross-border issues. Even those critical of the present system of multilateral financial assistance, such as the International Financial Advisory Commission to the United States Congress (the Meltzer Commission), have called on the multilateral financial institutions and other official bilateral donors to do more for the provision of IPGs. Indeed, Kanbur (2001a,b) argues that IPGs could potentially reverse the decline of official assistance observed in the 1990s, although he notes that such financing of IPGs should be judged by what it does for the poor in low-income countries rather than by the criterion of whether it enhances global welfare.

Tying the IPGs agenda to the system of official development finance greatly narrows its focus, because those engaged in development finance cannot typically influence the industrial nations to make the decisions required to supply the full range of IPGs. Climate change is an example. While official donor agencies can finance some of the investment developing countries need to facilitate carbon trading, the basic rules and infrastructure required for carbon trading require a broader consensus.

Thus even though they are being called upon to play a larger role in the provision of IPGs, there is some question whether the official donor agencies will be effective in doing so. Their main clients have tended to be sovereign governments, and the traditional system of official finance is largely built around assistance to individual countries. While this has changed in recent years with more lending and grants to subsovereign governments, nongovernmental organizations, and the private sector, national governments continue to limit the ability to coordinate projects and programs across countries. IPG provision has tended to occur on an ad hoc basis, often in response to highly visible emergencies, such as the emergence of AIDS and the occurrence of financial crises that spill across borders.

The limitations of traditional development assistance are one reason for the growing influence of a variety of formally and informally organized coalitions. These, according to Reinicke (2001), are flexible networks that bring together governments, civil society, and the private sector with international bureaucracies acting principally as facilitators. Reinicke (2001, p. 44) suggests: "Networks *address transnational issues that no single group can resolve by itself.* In many ways, globalization has changed power relationships. Neither multinational corporations nor civil society can be ignored in global public policymaking."

Therefore solutions to the provision of IPGs need to be viewed in the context of the evolving structure of global governance. While leader nations may sometimes provide IPGs unilaterally (see chapter 3 in this volume; Sandler 2001), they are only likely to do so when it is in their self-interest. International organizations can play an important role, but the long-established limits on their activities remain, restricting their financing actions largely to individual countries. The growing demand for IPGs provides an opportunity to make the case for additional aid resources, but perhaps channeled in new ways. Working with various networks, international financial institutions will, therefore, sometimes act as convenors, bringing stakeholders together to decide on appropriate action, while at other times they will defer to those with greater expertise and legitimacy.

This book addresses the strategic and practical challenges of fostering the supply of IPGs, paying particular attention to the financing of these goods. Its premise is that a more structured system is needed for the governance and financing of IPGs. While recognizing that achieving that goal may take time, the book outlines a three-pronged approach, elements of which have been applied before, sometimes with considerable success, for example, in the control of river blindness and in agricultural research. However, the full strategy is required, we believe, to achieve sustainable and inclusive globalization. The three elements of our recommended approach are as follows:

- *Improving incentives for responsible action.* The provision of most IPGs— including those aimed at preserving the global environment and maintaining international financial stability—depends on the actions of a multitude of individuals, businesses, and governments, all of whom value these goods differently. Long-run sustainability and cost-effectiveness require aligning the incentives of countries and their citizens with the global public interest through the use of standards, treaties, and regulatory mechanisms.

- *Integrating global and regional programs with country-based financing.*
  IPGs' significant potential contribution to development calls for coordination and synergy between national and transnational development efforts. Merely providing IPGs is not enough. The supporting infrastructure that enables poor countries to absorb and use these goods effectively is also needed. This places new demands on an already constrained pool of development financing. Ensuring the right level of, and balance between, locally focused efforts and IPGs is likely to require an increase in overall aid flows, as well as a commitment to high-quality programs.

- *Using public resources to leverage commercially motivated private money.*
  The only way to meet the large resource requirements is by leveraging scarce official funds and the funds charitable foundations make available with other resources. These funds should be used strategically to mobilize or "pull in" commercially motivated private financing. Good candidates for applying pull mechanisms are activities that offer the eventual prospect of a commercially-run business, for example, developing and distributing new drugs and vaccines, bridging the information technology gap between rich and poor countries, and increasing agricultural productivity in developing countries.

This chapter follows the structure of the book. It begins by reviewing the various concepts underlying the term public goods. It then discusses alternative governance structures and, especially, how new incentives could induce internationally responsible actions. Finally, it considers strategies for financing and the special role of international financial organizations.

DEFINING INTERNATIONAL PUBLIC GOODS

What exactly are IPGs? Given the recent popularity of this concept, there is a danger of the term being usurped for all manner of purposes, so that it loses both its analytical and practical significance. For example, poverty alleviation is sometimes described as an IPG. If that were so, almost all development activities would fall under the umbrella of IPGs, and the concept would have lost its edge. At the other extreme, as contributions to this book show, pinpointing exactly what is a public good is often difficult. Few goods fall into the category of pure public goods. Most are "impure" or mixed, displaying the characteristics of both private and public goods. A practical judgment has typically to be made in operationalizing the concept, which leads to a small, but significant and growing, set of development activities (see World Bank 2001; chapter 5). Box 1.1 lists those goods that can be reasonably considered IPGs and concludes that, while it is not useful to regard poverty reduction itself as an IPG, the IPGs we do consider can play an important role in reducing poverty.

In addition, besides the obvious semantic problem that a public good is not always a tangible good, but the elimination of a "bad," an important characteristic of some of the most important public goods is that they take the form of rules and institutions rather than benefits that provide direct utility.

Nonrivalry and Nonexcludability

Morrissey, te Velde, and Hewitt discuss the concept of IPGs in chapter 2. Starting from Samuelson's classical definition of a public good, the authors reflect on the meaning of both "international" and "public." They define an IPG as a benefit providing utility that is, in principle, available on an international scale. While they point to many difficulties in all three terms, "international," "public," and "good," they work with the traditional definition: IPGs are nonrival and nonexcludable across international borders.

Nonrivalry is the easier problem. My consumption of a particular good does not reduce your consumption. Nonrivalry raises the challenge of determining the optimal quantity of a public good: some form of cost-benefit calculation is required to determine how much of a particular good should be provided.

Nonexcludability is the source of coordination and financing problems in the provision of public goods because of the incentive to free-ride. As all countries benefit, all should contribute to the cost of providing IPGs, but the problem of valuation and of differences in countries' ability to pay can complicate matters. Different countries may place different values on certain public goods, leading to differences in their motivation to contribute to the supply of the goods, while their incomes and other factors affect their ability to contribute. The variation in the ability to contribute gives rise to the need for international transfers in the production of public goods, bringing to the fore

Box 1.1. How Can IPGs Help Reduce Poverty?

IPGs could yield a high payoff in terms of poverty reduction by improving outcomes in certain policy domains that are particularly relevant to developing countries. This would improve the effectiveness of aid.

- *Health.* Infectious diseases severely disrupt economic life in many developing countries. They kill many adults during their productive years, and the dislocation of families to escape these scourges reduces investment in child development. Even when disease does not kill or threaten to kill, it often reduces economic activity well below its potential. For example, malaria continues to impose a high cost through lost workdays.
- *Environment.* Many tropical developing countries are more vulnerable to projected climate change than countries in the temperate zones. Global warming is likely to affect food production in the tropics adversely and may increase the range of tropical contagious diseases. Some low-lying developing countries, such as Bangladesh, are also likely to be disproportionately affected if sea levels rise, because they lack the resources and infrastructure to cope with the resulting floods.
- *Knowledge.* Modern information and communications technologies have greatly enhanced developing countries' ability to tap into the global knowledge pool. These technologies help improve people's access to services and resources, thereby empowering them and expanding their economic opportunities. For example, biotechnology has improved plant varieties and the genetic potential of livestock, allowing more flexible crop management and boosting productivity. This may accelerate the reduction of rural poverty, which has recently slowed in a number of countries with a large number of poor.
- *Peace and security.* Conflict triggers instability and social dislocation, hampering growth and undoing progress in poverty reduction. As Africa's experience demonstrates, civil wars and domestic unrest can easily spread, destabilizing entire regions and limiting countries' abilities to share in the benefits of expanding world trade, financial flows, and technological advances.
- *Financial stability.* Boom and bust economic cycles prevent countries from consolidating progress in poverty reduction, because it is the poorest who are the most vulnerable to these swings. For example, evidence from metropolitan areas in Brazil shows recent large swings in the poverty rate, which edged up in the wake of the emerging market financial crisis and has fallen again since late 1999 thanks to the resumption of growth.

Although a number of global and regional endeavors to create IPGs entail considerable investment costs, others do not. For example, the chief input into the creation and promulgation of rules and standards to safeguard financial stability is negotiations, not capital. Such policy initiatives may therefore have even higher financial payoffs in terms of poverty reduction.

Source: World Bank (2001).

a new role for official development assistance (ODA) or foreign aid (multilateral and bilateral).

In chapter 3 Barrett discusses how coordination problems are resolved in local communities and within nations. In essence, the solution lies in a clearer definition of property rights, which then create private incentives to cooperate. In his classic contribution, Coase (1990) reviews the history of lighthouses in the United Kingdom and concludes that property rights were reasonably well defined and permitted a system of user fees (principally, a fixed entry fee) that funded lighthouses without extensive state intervention. However, Barrett argues that such a definition of property rights becomes progressively less useful as the spatial domain expands to include an increasing number of nations.

Morrissey, te Velde, and Hewitt reflect on another interesting definitional issue: what is the difference between externalities and public goods? In a recent contribution, Kanbur (2001b) uses both terms in the title of his paper, but then uses them synonymously in the text. The term externality refers to the consequences my actions may have for others for which they receive no financial compensation. We believe that the term cross-border externality is perhaps more descriptive of a problem that requires international attention, and that the term public good, with its more subtle connotations, is less easy to handle both analytically and operationally. But perhaps this ship has sailed. Morrissey, te Velde, and Hewitt, arguing through examples, conclude that while the problem originates, in the first instance, through externalities, the solution takes on the character of a public good. Thus when nations pollute, that has consequences for other nations for which they are not compensated. The polluted environment then becomes a public bad that requires public action.

Based on these considerations, Morrissey, te Velde, and Hewitt offer a classification of public goods. In the spirit of World Bank (2001), they conclude that several categories of public expenditures that relate to the environment, health, peacekeeping, knowledge generation and diffusion, and international governance are most closely related to public goods. They then classify the public goods into two categories: those that principally have national benefits and those that have international benefits.

Rules and Institutions

Rules and institutions are themselves public goods, and are key to the provision of IPGs. Indeed, they often better meet the criteria for nonrivalry and nonexcludability than do direct benefits arising, for example, from a cleaner environment and more research and development. Nonrivalry applies clearly to standards and with minor qualification to institutions. Nonexcludability, as always, is more problematic. Standards can be proprietary and institutions can close their doors to some would-be participants. Standards are seldom uncontroversial. A key problem with setting standards is that standard setting assumes knowledge of and consensus on a variety of matters. For example, economists disagree about the design of an efficient bankruptcy law and about whether fixed or flexible exchange rates are superior. Even the new guidelines for capital adequacy, which have key regulatory implications, invite controversy. However, a variety of standards and institutions have open accessibility.

Barrett, in chapter 3, considers the role of standards in helping achieve coordination in relation to achieving a cleaner environment. The role of financial standards is discussed in World Bank (2001), which also summarizes some of the growing literature on that subject. Sandler, in chapter 4, describes several international public institutions with varying degrees of accessibility that provide, for example, peacekeeping, communications, and development finance services.

Technology for Public Goods Production

The discussion above has focused on the nature of benefits and costs associated with IPGs. However, a cost-benefit analysis for their provision also requires knowledge of their production technology.

In this context it is useful to consider three types of IPGs, which Sandler discusses in detail in chapter 4 and are summarized here in table 1.1. Best shot goods, which depend on focused technical expertise and benefit from economies of scale, are organized for production and delivery in a centralized location or in a closely networked manner. Traditionally, such goods have been supplied through the so-called "push" model, with the public sector sponsoring the enterprise and assuming the full financial risk.

"Pull" measures operate by recognizing that the public sector continues to bear some of the responsibility for financing public goods even as it seeks to harness the private sector's flexibility and entrepreneurship. This is achieved by shifting some of the risk of product development to the private sector. Pull measures are not, however, conventional subsidies, but are more like contingent contracts. Payment is due only if services are delivered.

Table 1.1. Production Technologies of Public Goods: Institutional Implications

Supply technology	Examples	Institutional implications
Best shot: the most concerted effort determines the public good level	• Finding a cure for AIDS • Neutralizing a pest • Engineering the next green revolution	Incentives in the form of "prizes," or assured compensation, shift the risk of product development to the private sector. Requires complex public-private partnerships and supporting regulations.
Summation: the (weighted) sum of individual contributions determines the public good level	• Curbing air pollution • Reducing global warming • Cataloging species	Cannot typically rely on voluntary action at the national level. International treaties can create the property (trading) rights needed for provision of the public good, but also requires systems of taxes and penalties that limit the free-rider problem.
Weakest link: the smallest effort determines the public good level	• Containing river blindness • Limiting the spread of insurrections • Achieving international financial stability	Capacity building required in poor countries. Partnerships among various participants can circumvent collective action problems. Incentives are critical to limit moral hazard (cheating) that puts others at risk.

Source: Adapted from chapter 4 in this volume.

In contrast, summation and weakest link goods, which depend on the actions and contributions of widely dispersed individuals, are not generally suitable for either the push or the pull approach. Instead, such goods require a wide set of global partnerships. Official agencies essentially play a catalytic role, and the pragmatic mobilization of global coalitions through informal partnerships, standards, and treaties becomes more prominent.

INCENTIVES FOR RESPONSIBLE ACTION

When global outcomes result from the uncoordinated actions of many individuals, institutions, and governments, the unintended consequences can sometimes be financially serious, but additional financial resources do not always help achieve the needed coordination. Coordinated action requires incentives, not just for the sake of efficiency, but also for inclusiveness. Establishing incentives for governments, nongovernmental entities, the business sector, and individuals to act in the global interest lies at the core of providing IPGs. Measures to contain global warming and maintain financial stability and the international trade regime are some of the most prominent examples where international coordination is critical.

The policy goal is to establish rules of the game that promote efficiency, transparency, and equity in access. To that end, the global community uses a variety of devices, including standards, treaties, and supporting regulations. This section first follows Barrett's arguments in chapter 3 to highlight the constraints on effective coordination through these mechanisms. However, it then goes on to suggest where the possibilities for coordination may lie. It follows Barrett in exploring the idea of a "tipping" balance. When a sufficient number of parties agree to a course of action, then the balance can quickly shift from a lack of cooperation to a cooperative outcome. To this end, this section explores the current constraints underlying the Kyoto Protocol on global warming and concludes that a learning process is ongoing, which could achieve coordinated outcomes in the future. Similarly, the recent emergence of a variety of global coalitions in the form of advocacy and action groups could also help achieve a critical level of cooperation.

The Constraints to International Coordination

Cooperation in the supply of IPGs—on a global or regional scale—is often expressed in an international treaty or agreement, supported by the required institutions, for example, a treaty secretariat and, possibly, arrangements for side payments. Treaties can set rules of the game in a way that is more binding than standards, but with a few important exceptions, such as fisheries treaties and the Montreal Protocol for Ozone Reduction, they have been difficult to accomplish. Regulatory oversight of global activities has succeeded in some areas, such as air traffic control, but has been more contentious in others, such as international antitrust and competition policy.

Barrett, in chapter 3, identifies why international cooperation is difficult, using the concepts of game theory. He argues that international treaties are extremely difficult to enforce, because they almost always allow a country to opt out. He then asks if trade linkages, which are based on reciprocal relations, can be used to enforce treaties and is pessimistic on this score. Instead of the "stick" of trade sanctions, the "carrot" of financial compensation may sometimes work, but again, Barrett is not optimistic.

A country's interests in influencing the supply of global and regional public goods depends on what other countries are doing, therefore treaty design must take this strategic interdependence into account. Barrett explores many of the implications that flow from this observation. For example, where strategic interdependence exists, negative and positive feedback is possible. With negative feedback, as one country increases its supply of the public good, others have an incentive to reduce their supply. In contrast, with positive feedback, some may have an incentive to increase their supply.

Barrett notes that a supranational government backed by the power to tax could remedy the mismatch of demand for and supply of IPGs, but because no such entity exists, the commitment of public and private resources to IPGs requires the coordination of efforts across national borders, a process that is often slow and difficult to enforce. Barrett notes also that successful treaties have typically depended upon the interests of a single nation or a few nations for whom the obligations under the treaty were beneficial, almost no matter how the other countries chose to proceed. He cites the Montreal Protocol for Ozone Layer Depletion as an example where the strong U.S. interest created the necessary condition for the treaty to be established.

On a more hopeful note, Barrett's analysis shows that in the presence of positive feedback coupled with a threshold effect, a tipping point may exist, such that with the agreement of a critical mass of nations, the incentives to join the treaty are increased for the nonparticipating nations. The global system of trading rules achieved under successive rounds of multilateral negotiations is an example. Starting principally with a small group of industrial nations, over time an increasingly larger group of countries has become party to the obligations under these rules. Moreover, even though the system embodies a set of reciprocal obligations, and hence the possibility of reciprocal sanctions, countries have increasingly come to accept something close to an economist's ideal: the merits of unilateral trade liberalization.

The Kyoto Protocol: The First Stage of a Learning Curve?

Even though disastrous consequences resulting from global warming are low-probability events, their costs, if they transpired, could be catastrophically high, and would also be disproportionately borne by the poor. Therefore, pursuant to the precautionary principle, the global community has a strong interest in mitigating these risks, and despite the controversies that have arisen, progress to date demonstrates that the coordination of incentives can be achieved in an evolutionary way. Currently the main approach to reducing global warming, embodied in the 1997 Kyoto Protocol, establishes quantitative limits by country on its emission of the greenhouse gases responsible for warming: signatories to the protocol are required to reduce their greenhouse gas emissions at least 5 percent by 2008–12. While many elements of the protocol are subject to criticism, it is a necessary step toward a global governance system for managing the risks of global warming. The many experiments currently under way could create the necessary basis for a substantive agreement.

A special feature of the Kyoto Protocol is its Clean Development Mechanism, which provides for the possibility of international trade in emission rights. Such trade would contribute to efficiency in reducing emissions, and could also transfer significant resources from industrial to developing countries. If trading rights function effectively, the marginal cost of eliminating a ton of carbon emissions could fall from US$200 to US$23 (Cooper 2000). However, some consider the protocol as a whole to be both inefficient and unworkable (Cooper 2000; Nordhaus and Boyer 1998; chapter 3 in this volume).

Despite the provision for trading, however, Nordhaus and Boyer (1998) conclude that the approach is inefficient, because the benchmark emission reductions set for different countries are arbitrary and will not lead to a globally optimal mix of reductions. Moreover, about two-thirds of the costs would fall on the United States, which because of the macroeconomic implications is unlikely to support the protocol. Others criticize the Kyoto Protocol for being difficult to monitor (Cooper 2000) and for its weak treaty. However, despite its weaknesses, new ideas and practices are emerging from experience with the negotiation of the Kyoto Protocol, which could lead to a more acceptable and workable system.

The immediate prospects of international trade in pollution rights under the Clean Development Mechanism are not bright, but the idea's eventual promise makes this an important experiment. Under the mechanism, industrial countries that have committed to reduce their greenhouse gas emissions could purchase rights to emit greenhouse gases from activities in developing countries that hold emission rights. Emission rights trading is intended to ensure that emissions reductions occur where they are cheapest to implement.

The Kyoto Protocol is unclear about exactly how such reductions would be measured and certified. This is a crucial impediment. However, if the mechanism could be made to work, the resulting resource transfers to developing countries could be US$5 billion to US$10 billion a year (Black and others 2000). The major beneficiaries would be China, India, and Russia, but other countries would also benefit.[2] For Colombia, sales of pollution permits could raise revenues equal to those from exports of bananas or cut flowers (Black and others 2000). Collateral benefits in the form of higher rural wages, higher employment, greater technology transfers, and reduced air and water pollution could add to the development impact (Austin and Faeth 2000; Black and others 2000). The Prototype Carbon Fund, a private-public partnership sponsored by the World Bank, aims to facilitate emissions rights transactions between private investors and host countries (see Newcombe 2001 for details). By monitoring emissions reduction, verification, and certification, the fund could help build trust between the parties from an early stage. Such trust is necessary for sound development of the market. The fund also expects to attract additional public and private resources and promote the transfer of environmentally safe technologies. The Prototype Carbon Fund is an example of networks that could help increase coordination across national borders.

Networks for Fostering Coalitions

In the absence of a central authority to ensure coordination, can informal coalitions of stakeholders serve a constructive function? The spontaneous growth of global coalitions that can be observed today is a favorable development. These networks of nongovernmental and governmental actors carry some of the burden of building constituencies for coordinated action. Multilateral organizations can play a critical convening function and a role as catalysts and supporters of coalitions to provide IPGs.

Reinicke (2001, p. 43) states that these trilateral alliances among governments, civil society, and the private sector serve to "internalize the changing global environment, especially the basic value of deeper integration of the world economy." By bringing together complementary strengths, they help "address transnational issues that no single group can resolve itself." However, as Picciotto (1995) has emphasized, global networks are effective when their organization reflects the characteristics of the public good in question.

Alliances have been used extensively in the corporate world, where they serve two functions: reducing transactions costs and fostering a learning process (see Mody 1993). In a corporate environment, as in global public policy, transaction costs occur when markets lack sufficient information, and hence dysfunctional actions on the part of the various actors involved are possible. In principle, when the incentives to share complementary information can be created, an alliance can reduce information gaps, but the main gains are unlikely to lie in a one-shot sharing of information. Alliances' ability to achieve coordination is likely to occur principally when they can experiment with innovative approaches. The learning processes that unfold as a result can help identify, and even create, conditions under which cooperation becomes more attractive to the various parties. Balanced against these benefits are the obvious costs that arise if alliances generate restricted clubs. In the corporate world, this leads to concerns about the creation and exercise of market power. In the policy world, the concern lies with the creation of rules and institutions that serve to exclude rather than include.

Policy networks can serve several functions. They can, for example, advocate special causes, but they can go further and help negotiate and set global standards (Reinicke 2001). An example that illustrates the potential for networks is the World Commission on Dams. The commission was charged with the sensitive task of proposing standards that could meet multiple objectives: furthering economic growth, protecting the environment, and ensuring a fair deal to those who are displaced or otherwise hurt by the construction of the dam. The commission brought together political and economic leaders from across the globe. Multilateral institutions such as the World Bank worked mainly to facilitate the process. In the event, the progress achieved was perhaps limited and the challenges remain; however, as with the Kyoto Protocol, such efforts are early steps in confronting complex tradeoffs.

INTEGRATING COUNTRY-BASED FINANCING AND GLOBAL AND REGIONAL PROGRAMS

The financing of IPGs raises a series of questions. What do we know about the trends in the financing of IPGs? Are these trends largely beneficial, or are there underlying risks against which policymakers need to be vigilant? Looking ahead, is a centralized pool of funding to finance IPGs something to think about? What types of financing arrangements would make the most effective use of scarce public resources? What should the role of international financial institutions be in furthering the financing of IPGs?

International Development Assistance for IPGs

The provision of IPGs calls for policies and financing at various jurisdictional levels ranging from the local to the global. At this time, we simply do not know how much aggregate funding occurs for IPGs. We do have a somewhat better idea about a narrower question: the extent of official financing by multilateral and bilateral donors that directly or indirectly facilitates the creation of IPGs in developing countries (see World Bank 2001, chapter 4). Such financing does not, of course, include the financing of IPGs undertaken in the industrial countries. Thus, for example, the annual budget of the U.S. Environmental Protection Agency is about US$10 billion dollars, much of which potentially provides an IPG; all ODA directed toward environmental IPGs is about one-tenth of the U.S. Environmental Protection Agency's budget. However, official financing also omits the IPGs financed by developing countries without international assistance and expenditures incurred by multilateral agencies but not financed by the conventional aid budget. Thus, for example, funding of United Nations peacekeeping forces is not reflected in official financing statistics, which therefore show a smaller amount devoted to matters related to safeguarding of peace than is the case in reality (see World Bank 2001).

Yet despite these limitations, trends in the official financing of IPGs are important not only because of the implications for the effectiveness of such financing, but also because these trends are likely to reflect broader global priorities.

Core and Complementary Activities

In the empirical discussion that follows, an important distinction in made between core and complementary activities. Core activities aim to produce IPGs. These activities include global and regional programs, as well as activities that are focused in one country, but whose benefits spill over to others. Examples of multicountry programs include carrying out international agricultural research; creating incentives to achieve breakthroughs in medical technology; and holding negotiations to develop rules and standards, such as the bank solvency proposals the Basle committee of financial regulators advanced in early 2001. An example of a country-focused activity with positive spillovers is an effective epidemiological policy to combat a disease in one country that also reduces neighboring countries' exposure to that disease.

By contrast, complementary activities prepare countries to consume the IPGs that core activities make available, while at the same time creating valuable national public goods. Traditional country-based financial flows to support domestic policy, institutional reform, and investment in infrastructure are primarily motivated by the benefits expected within the country, but these flows and the national public goods they help create may also enhance the country's ability to absorb the benefits of IPGs. For example, a country cannot use international agricultural research goods effectively in the absence of adequate domestic agricultural services and incentives. Thus core and complementary activities interact. For the best results, they must go hand in hand.

Trends in International Resource Transfers for IPGs

International resource transfers for core activities amount to about US$5 billion a year (table 1.2). Sources with a global or regional mandate provide US$3 billion a year, typically as grants—private charitable foundations contribute about $1 billion and the rest is channeled by official donors through a variety of trust funds. In addition, country-based concessional aid (grants and loans with a grant component of more than 25 percent, commonly referred to simply as "aid" and more formally as ODA) finances transfers in the amount of US$2 billion for those national public goods that, like peacekeeping, also have cross-border implications.

Table 1.2. Sources of Funding for IPGs and Complementary Activities, Annual Averages, 1995–99

(US$ billions)

Category	Global and regional funding		Country-based financing		
	Foundations	Trust funds	Concessional	Non-concessional	Total
IPGs ("core" goods)	1	2	2	0	5
Complementary goods	0	0	8	3	11
Total	1	2	10	3	16

Source: World Bank (2001) based on The Foundation Center (1997, 2001); Development Assistance Committee of the Organisation for Economic Co-operation and Development data.

An additional US$11 billion a year is spent on complementary activities that fund domestic mechanisms and the infrastructure that allow countries to absorb the benefits of these IPGs. Thus, for example, funding is needed to build domestic public health infrastructure so that countries can benefit from such IPGs as drugs and vaccines to control infectious diseases; and environmental education, training, and administrative capacity are needed at the local level to complement international agreements to reduce pollution. These complementary activities are funded in large part by concessional funds (US$8 billion), and in part by nonconcessional lending from multilateral financial institutions (US$3 billion).

The Role of Aid: Official Development Assistance

Although philanthropic assistance is important and likely to grow (World Bank 2001), as is nonconcessional official assistance, the bulk of funding comes through concessional assistance or ODA. In the second half of the 1990s ODA contributed about US$2 billion a year toward core IPG spending. As a fraction of total ODA, spending on IPGs rose from about 1.5 percent in the 1970s to 3.5 percent in the late 1990s (figure 1.1). In 1999 core spending reached nearly 8 percent of ODA, largely reflecting increased expenditure for peacekeeping operations. Funding for health, the environment, and peacekeeping has grown significantly, while that for knowledge generation and dissemination has stagnated.

A far more significant part of ODA—estimated at about US$8 billion a year in the late 1990s—is channeled to complementary expenditure. This component rose from about 6 percent of all ODA in the 1970s to more than 15 percent in the late 1990s. These expenditures have been relatively resilient in the face of declining aid flows since the mid-1990s. They are particularly important in the health domain, where the control of infectious diseases requires significant supporting infrastructure.

In chapter 5, te Velde, Morrissey, and Hewitt present a detailed analysis of spending by official donors on IPGs. The authors classify public goods into five "sectors": environment, health, knowledge, governance, and conflict prevention or security. Building on the analysis of World Bank (2001), they prefer to divide public goods into international and domestic categories. While these match the core and complementary distinctions to a significant extent—both in levels and trends—as the authors explain, some differences are apparent. These authors also examine the behavior of specific donors with regard to the financing of IPGs and find a generally rising trend.

Figure 1.1. Share of Development Assistance Allocated to IPGs, 1970–99

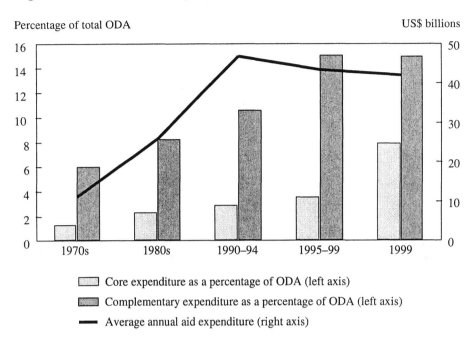

Percentage of total ODA ··· US$ billions

Core expenditure as a percentage of ODA (left axis)
Complementary expenditure as a percentage of ODA (left axis)
Average annual aid expenditure (right axis)

Source: World Bank staff estimates.

Te Velde, Morrissey, and Hewitt also ask if the increasing share of resources that have been directed to the provision of IPGs has come at the expense of other forms of aid. Until the early 1990s, while expenditures on IPGs grew, so apparently did expenditures on all other aid. However, the continued increase in spending on IPGs in the 1990s took place in an environment of declining overall aid, implying that IPG spending is displacing other expenditures. They conclude, however, that spending on national public goods in the five sectors they consider also grew in the 1990s. Thus IPGs and national public goods grew, while other traditional forms of aid declined.

Regional Public Goods

In chapter 6 Ferroni examines the financing of regional public goods. His analysis agrees with Barrett's that regional public goods may be easier to supply than global public goods. All else being equal, the incentives to free-ride increase with the number of countries that must supply a public good. Given the growth in the number of regional trade agreements during the past decade, Ferroni infers that the demand for regional public goods is rising. The pursuit of commercial integration gradually leads to cooperation in policy domains beyond trade, including infrastructure (an area of cross-border cooperation not addressed here or in chapter 5), finance, public health, environmental codes and standards, and other areas. However, he notes that joint action by countries in a region is neither straightforward nor easy, despite the growing interest in regional integration worldwide.

Ferroni focuses on the role of the multilateral development banks in supplying and financing regional public goods. He argues that these institutions are increasingly engaged in working with their borrowing member governments to supply regional public goods and analyzes how the banks' lending and nonlending operations are financing regional public goods. With reference to the core versus complementary distinction, he clarifies the types of public goods-related activities that can be funded by means of loans, specifies those instances where the less abundant resource of grants is appropriate, and outlines some of the pitfalls that can accompany grant financing.

Can—and Should—Additional Official Resources Be Devoted to IPGs?

While no estimate exists for the resources required for IPGs, the presumption often is that significant additional resources could be effectively used. For example, the United Nations Special Session on HIV/AIDS concluded: "An overall annual expenditure target of US$7–10 billion in low- and middle-income countries must be reached to mount a comprehensive and successful response to HIV/AIDS. The shortage of resources to fight tuberculosis and malaria stands at about US$2 billion a year" (see http://www.un.org/ga/aids/ungassfactsheets/html/ fsfund_en.htm). Clearly these sums are large not only in relation to official resource transfers for IPGs, but also in relation to the overall aid flows to developing countries.

In the case of other IPGs, the demand for additional resources is more controversial. For example, with respect to global warming, Schelling (1997) argues that the benefits will largely accrue to future generations, who will also be richer, and who should, therefore, bear the cost. Thus scarce resources should be used to finance current more pressing needs. In chapter 4 Sandler urges caution in the enthusiasm for expanded financing of IPGs. He notes that the examples of pure public goods are few, and that institutional arrangements can often be achieved to create "club" goods, which can then generate revenues necessary for the financing of such goods.

Kanbur (2001a) believes that IPGs help justify more aid. To him, global demand for more IPGs justifies additional aid, though such additional aid may best finance traditional (in our terminology, complementary) expenditures, such as health delivery systems. He notes, however, that in some instances shifting existing aid expenditures to the industrial countries for the provision of core public goods may be desirable. Thus research and development (R&D) in relation to certain knowledge products may be most efficiently conducted in industrial countries.

Cooper (2001, p. 22) cautions that even if the case for significantly stepped-up resources could be made, the prospects for doing so are not good. Reviewing the evidence for proposals to create an international pool of resources that could be used for financing IPGs, he notes that either the proposals were not based on sound principles, or the amounts involved were small, or, most important, the political consensus to implement the proposals simply did not exist. In practice, he concludes, the answer to the question: "Are there any prospects for developing fully *international* sources of finance for global public goods?" is no, because of "the attitude of governments and their public towards taxes."

The problem of added resources may ultimately be solved in unconventional ways. Lancaster (2000) argues that political support does exist in the United States for devoting more resources to global problems, but that these resources are being channeled in new ways that reflect the objectives of either directly dealing with the poor or mediating aid through the private sector. The U.S. tax credit for development of an AIDS vaccine is an example of funds made available, but not transferred through traditional channels. Tax incentives for charitable giving similarly enlarge the resource envelope. These and other shifts imply that in the aid business, it will not be business as usual.

Thus both the rationale and prospects for a general enhancement of resources for IPGs remain clouded. For this reason, while the importance of ensuring adequate funding for specific purposes, such as dealing with HIV/AIDS, cannot be minimized—and, indeed, scarce available resources should be used to their maximum potential—the continuing emphasis must be on generating incentives at the local level for activities that contribute to IPGs.

Leveraging Official and Philanthropic Resources

Private foundation and official resources are scarce, and the claims on their use are many. Leveraging these resources can expand the envelope of funds available to provide IPGs. The goal of such leveraging is to attract commercially-oriented resources, but because of the financial risks involved in the provision of such goods, private funding may not be forthcoming. Pull mechanisms operate not by subsidizing activities in the traditional manner, but by assuring sales contingent on the successful development of the public good in question. Such leveraging is most likely in the development of vaccines and new agricultural technology, but possibly also in narrowing the digital divide. In these contexts a key technological development is often required that, in turn, implies the deployment of significant dedicated resources. By offering the "prize" of an assured minimal market, the private sector can sometimes be motivated to devote its own resources to the risky development phase. The chronometer to solve the longitude problem and the means to control cholera were both the results of prize competitions (Cooper 2001). Pull mechanisms through contingent contracts can be both effective and efficient, because they pay for the output of research (the public good itself), not for the inputs (Kremer 2000).

The push approach has traditionally been used for best shot public goods that require a high degree of technical expertise and where high fixed costs of production are associated with significant technical and market risks (see table 1.1). Knowledge and knowledge infrastructure are best shot public goods, of which the Internet is an example. The U.S. Department of Defense and its Advanced Research Projects Agency created the Internet. Its use exploded through private initiative once the network and its protocols had been established, and could be greatly enhanced through an initial push on portals and navigation standards for developing country communities. Such a push could not only fund early fixed costs, but could also generate demonstration effects that subsequently pull in new private initiatives.

Because the incidence of HIV/AIDS is highest in many developing countries with a low ability to pay, the incentives to invest in R&D are weak, as the developer may not be able to directly recoup the costs.[3] Low purchasing power and low childhood immunization rates create the presumption on the part of pharmaceutical companies that the market for an AIDS vaccine in developing countries would not be large enough to warrant the investment. Even though the cost of all four basic childhood vaccines is less than US$1 per child, coverage remains low in the poorest countries, and an AIDS vaccine is likely to be much more expensive.

Recent push mechanisms for vaccines have operated through networks of governmental and nongovernmental organizations, with representation from the private sector. The Medicines for Malaria Venture, the International AIDS Vaccine Initiative, and similar networks draw funds from private foundations and official trust funds to finance vaccine and drug development (for details, see World Bank 2001).

Other pull approaches are under consideration. Under a U.S. government proposal, every US$1 of vaccine sales would be matched by a US$1 tax credit.[4] Setting up an HIV vaccine purchase fund financed by donors and developing countries would also signal the commitment to pay for a vaccine and would stimulate private sector research. A replenishing fund has been proposed using International Development Association (IDA) resources and other multilateral concessional funds (Ainsworth and others 1999). Providing contingent loans and guarantees to developing countries to purchase a vaccine that would meet donors' standards is another option to stimulate private sector R&D. By creating a greater likelihood of vaccine use, traditional country-based programs can also pull the development of vaccines.

Some major uncertainties surround global pull initiatives, however. Is the international community willing to lock in large amounts of capital for a long time if this means reducing the availability of resources for other development priorities? Will the promise of funds be credible enough to bring about the necessary research effort? Will the processes for evaluating whether countries qualify to receive such funds be simple enough to minimize disputes? These uncertainties reveal why country-specific development assistance and policy dialogue should continue.[5] Indeed, by building the infrastructure needed to deliver vaccines and provide supporting medical and sanitation services, such country programs may exert the strongest pull on vaccine development.

The New Challenges for International Organizations

International organizations have been central to the provision of public goods through their resources, their knowledge transfers, and their global negotiations and rule making (Kapur 2000). They also generate information; lower the cost of transactions; encourage members to think about a common future; create links across issues; and create and diffuse ideas, norms, and expectations (Martin and Simmons 1998; Ruggie 1992). In addition, they negotiate and manage rules for conditionality, sanctions, and even the use of direct force (as in the case of the North Atlantic Treaty Organization). International organizations are themselves IPGs (see chapter 4 in this volume).

Thus international organizations are critical to the three-pronged approach to IPGs advocated in this chapter: in their catalytic role in convening stakeholders and providing platforms for international joint action, as conduits for funding investments (both for the core and complementary activities) that their clients undertake, and in the creation of the frameworks to leverage public resources with private funds. However, significant challenges lie ahead. In light of the foregoing discussion, it is not clear that international organizations will be able to deploy more resources unless a significant change occurs in the international aid environment. Linked to the question of more aid is the ability of all donors to use their funds more efficiently, a challenge that does not go away with the move from traditional expenditures toward IPGs. At the same time, to function effectively themselves, international organizations need to better coordinate with each other, observing the principle of subsidiarity. They could also achieve greater effectiveness by deploying innovative financial instruments; however, we would caution against the search for more finely-tuned financial instruments unless set in the context of genuine project opportunities.

Making larger aid budgets available to international organizations and to all donors could significantly boost priority areas, such as vaccines and drugs for diseases that disproportionately affect the poor. However, additional spending on a significant scale risks damaging existing country programs and complementary expenditures. While more funds may be available, they may not be routed through the traditional international organizations. At the same time, the concern also exists about how efficiently aid resources are used. Both more funds and new incentive frameworks for effective aid deployment are needed, as are improved mechanisms for aid coordination (World Bank 2001, chapter 4). The IPGs agenda opens up new, and heretofore little explored, dimensions of aid coordination that relate to timing, balance, and synergy between core and complementary activities.

International organizations must be willing to observe the principle of subsidiarity: allowing the most effective organization in any given initiative to take the lead. They must partner with others to establish priorities, set standards, and use demonstration projects to create knowledge for action. The discussion of such coalition-based governance and the meaning of subsidiarity in this context is still at an early stage. It will need to evolve in the context of an appropriate, yet still to be identified, framework for achieving effective policymaking in a decentralized stakeholder setting. By operating in a network-based system of governance, international organizations will influence political decisionmaking to advance global interests.

Ferroni, in chapter 6, is cautious about the proposal for differentially pricing loans for IPGs, because that does not expand the envelope of resources. In theory, differential pricing would permit fine-tuning of subsidies for different kinds of IPGs, but it could also be difficult to administer, with administration likely becoming a politically charged exercise.

In the absence of differential pricing, loans will need to be combined with grant funding in appropriate combinations to foster the production of some public goods that spill across borders. This is already being done in the form of hybrid financial products that combine concessional or nonconcessional lending (depending on the type of borrower) and grant-based co-financing. The question is where will the full measure of needed grant funding come from? Possible answers include bilateral donors and transfers financed by increased charges on ordinary capital loans extended by the multilateral development banks. Neither of these options looks promising today. The financing of IPGs requiring public funding beyond current levels is therefore likely to depend on ad hoc arrangements for some time.

CONCLUSIONS

The already difficult task of providing IPGs is embedded in the even more complex evolution of global governance structures accompanying the process of globalization. National governments, international organizations, and the new networks that join these traditional sources of authority with civil society and the private sector will guide the provision of IPGs. The incentives for the generation and delivery of IPGs—reflected in international standards, regulations, and treaties—should ideally be set by the principles of economic efficiency and equity; however, it is the broader governance process that determines which incentives are put in place. Many economists believe, for example, that carbon taxation is superior to the quantitative emission limits proposed under the Kyoto Protocol. However, the political ability to implement such taxation does not exist at the present time. As such, the most fruitful approach is likely to be one that is not committed to a single course of action. Rather, multiple experiments in local and global contexts are likely to help illuminate what will work in practice.

The challenges of financing IPGs arise from the features that distinguish public goods from private ones, and also because of differences in the national and international taxation environments. National governments, either directly, or indirectly through their contributions to international organizations, are the principal sources of finance for IPGs. Much has been written about the scope for truly international sources of funding for public goods: the Tobin tax, the carbon tax, International Monetary Fund gold, and so on. In practice, and for many reasons (some of which are controversial), this scope is currently limited. Thus the supply of IPGs will largely continue to depend on governments' willingness and ability to devote national resources under their control to international purposes and goals. Significant contributions from charitable organizations augment official resources, and both must increasingly be leveraged by commercially motivated private money for some IPGs and for private goods and services that generate desirable cross-border externalities.

The multilateral financial institutions have come to recognize the growing importance of IPGs to their mission. This places new challenges before them, given that they have traditionally operated on a country-by-country basis. However, the pursuit of development and poverty reduction calls for policies and interventions at levels ranging from the local to the global. Thus even though the country focus continues to be important, it must be complemented by regional and global problem solving to counter undesirable cross-border spillovers and create a better environment for shared opportunities and growth. The multilateral organizations are uniquely placed to foster synergy and complementarity between country-level and transnationally focused action.

NOTES

1. This chapter draws on the authors' contributions to World Bank (2001, chapter 5). The authors would like to thank Christopher Gerrard, Ravi Kanbur, Robert Picciotto, and Todd Sandler for their comments on the chapter.

2. Other estimates predict much larger financial flows between countries, either as counterparts of permit transactions or as compensatory side payments (OECD 1999). Moderate abatement strategies would generate annual flows of about US$50 billion (in 1995 dollars), whereas more ambitious abatement paths could generate as much as US$150 billion to US$200 billion annually.

3. Total R&D expenditure on HIV vaccines was only about US$300 million in 1999, compared with an estimated US$2 billion spent annually on research for AIDS treatment and targeted to industrial country markets (Ainsworth and others 2000).

4. Unlike conventional tax credits that match R&D dollars spent, this credit would be available only when sales have been achieved. Qualifying vaccines would include those that prevent diseases causing at least 1 million deaths every year and would require regulatory approval (see Kremer 2000).

5. About 30 percent of IDA operations in health, nutrition, and population (which, on average, accounted for 15 percent of IDA investment lending in 1998–99) were directed at family and reproductive health, especially increasing immunizations and providing information on good health practices. IDA is the largest financier of tuberculosis control efforts in developing countries, with major operations in China and India. IDA is also a cofounder of the Global Initiative to Roll Back Malaria, launched in 1998 with the aim of halving deaths from malaria by 2010.

REFERENCES

The word *processed* describes informally reproduced works that may not be commonly available through libraries.

Ainsworth, M., A. Baston, G. Lamb, and S. Rosenhouse. 1999. "Accelerating an AIDS Vaccine for Developing Countries: Recommendations for the World Bank." Washington, D.C. Processed.

————. 2000. "Fostering Investment in Global Public Goods in Health: The Case of Communicable Diseases." In World Bank, *New Paths to Social Development: Community and Global Networks in Action*. Washington, D.C.: World Bank.

Austin, D., and P. Faeth. 2000. *Financing Sustainable Development with the Clean Development Mechanism: An Overview.* Washington, D.C.: World Resources Institute.

Black, T., and others. 2000. "National Strategy Study for Implementation of the CDM in Colombia: Executive Summary." Bogota: National Strategy Studies, Ministerio del Medio Ambiente, and World Bank.

Coase, Ronald. 1990. *The Firm, the Market, and the Law.* Chicago: The University of Chicago Press.

Cooper, R. 2000. "International Approaches to Global Climate Change." *World Bank Research Observer* 15(2): 145–73.

————. 2001. "Global Public Goods: A Historical Overview and New Challenges." In Christopher Gerrard, Marco Ferroni, and Ashoka Mody, eds., *Global Public Policies and Programs: Implications for Financing and Evaluation.* Proceedings from a World Bank workshop. Washington, D.C.: World Bank, Operations Evaluation Department.

Foundation Center, The, in cooperation with the Council on Foundations. 1997. *International Grantmaking: A Report on U.S. Foundation Trends.* Washington, D.C.

————. 2001. *International Grantmaking II: An Update on U.S. Foundation Trends.* Washington, D.C.

International Financial Institutions Advisory Commission. 2000. "Meltzer Commission Report." Washington, D.C. Available at: phantom-x.gsia.cmu.edu/IFIAC/Report.html.

Kanbur, Ravi. 2001a. "The Intersection of Development Assistance and International Public Goods." In Christopher Gerrard, Marco Ferroni, and Ashoka Mody, eds., *Global Public Policies and Programs: Implications for Financing and Evaluation.* Proceedings from a World Bank workshop. Washington, D.C.: World Bank, Operations Evaluation Department.

————. 2001b. "Cross-Border Externalities, International Public Goods and Their Implications for Aid Agencies." Ithaca, New York: Cornell University. Available at: http://www.people.cornell.edu/pages/sk145/papers/IPGWB.pdf.

Kanbur, R., T. Sandler, with K. Morrison. 1999. *The Future of Development Assistance: Common Pools and International Public Goods.* Policy Essay no. 25. Washington, D.C.: Overseas Development Council.

Kapur, D. 2000. "Burden Sharing and International Public Goods: Lessons from the World Bank's Net Income and Reserves." Harvard University, Cambridge, Massachusetts. Processed.

Kaul, I. 2001. "Six Reasons for a Global Public Goods Perspective on Development." In Christopher Gerrard, Marco Ferroni, and Ashoka Mody, eds., *Global Public Policies and Programs: Implications for Financing and Evaluation.* Proceedings from a World Bank workshop. Washington, D.C.: World Bank, Operations Evaluation Department.

Kaul, I., I. Grunberg, and M. Stern, eds. 1999. *Global Public Goods: International Cooperation in the 21st Century.* New York and Oxford: Oxford University Press.

Kindleberger, C. P. 1986. "International Public Goods without International Government." *American Economic Review* 76(1): 1–13.

Kremer, M. 2000. "Creating Markets for New Vaccines—Part II: Design Issue." Working Paper no. 7717. National Bureau of Economic Research, Cambridge, Massachusetts.

Lancaster, C. 2000. "Redesigning Foreign Aid." *Foreign Affairs* (September/October): 74–89.

Martin, L. L., and B. A. Simmons. 1998. "Theories and Empirical Studies of International Institutions." *International Organization* 52(4): 729–57.

Mody, A. 1993. "Learning through Alliances." *Journal of Economic Behavior and Organization* 20: 150–73.

Newcombe, K. 2001. "The Prototype Carbon Fund: Mobilizing Private and Public Resources to Combat Climate Change." In Christopher Gerrard, Marco Ferroni, and Ashoka Mody, eds., *Global Public Policies and Programs: Implications for Financing and Evaluation.* Proceedings from a World Bank workshop. Washington, D.C.: World Bank, Operations Evaluation Department.

Nordhaus, W. D., and J. G. Boyer. 1998. "Requiem for Kyoto: An Economic Analysis of the Kyoto Protocol." Cowles Foundation Discussion Paper no. 121. Yale University, New Haven, Connecticut.

OECD (Organisation for Economic Co-operation and Development). 1999. *Action against Climate Change: The Kyoto Protocol and Beyond.* Paris.

Picciotto, Robert. 1995. *Putting Institutional Economics to Work: From Participation to Governance.* Discussion Paper no. 304. Washington, D.C.: World Bank.

Reinicke, Wolfgang. 2001. "Walking the Talk: Global Public Policy in Action." In Christopher Gerrard, Marco Ferroni, and Ashoka Mody, eds., *Global Public Policies and Programs: Implications for Financing and Evaluation.* Proceedings from a World Bank workshop. Washington, D.C.: World Bank, Operations Evaluation Department.

Ruggie, J. G. 1992. "Multilateralism: The Anatomy of an Institution." *International Organization* 46(3): 561–98.

Sachs, J. 2000. "A New Map of the World." *The Economist.* June 24.

————. 2001. "What Is Good for the Poor Is Good for America." *Economist.* July 14.

Sandler, T. 1997. *Global Challenges: An Approach to Environmental, Political, and Economic Problems.* Cambridge, U.K.: Cambridge University Press.

———. 2001. "Financing Global and International Public Goods." In Christopher Gerrard, Marco Ferroni, and Ashoka Mody, eds., *Global Public Policies and Programs: Implications for Financing and Evaluation.* Proceedings from a World Bank workshop. Washington, D.C.: World Bank, Operations Evaluation Department.

Schelling, T. 1997. "The Costs of Global Warming." *Foreign Affairs* (November/December): 8–14.

Soros, George. Forthcoming. *The Soros Report on Globalization.* New York: Soros Fund Management.

Summers, L. 2000. "Development and Integration: Towards the New Global Consensus." Remarks to the United Nations Economic and Social Council, July 5, New York.

World Bank. 2001. *Global Development Finance: Building Coalitions for Effective Development Finance.* Washington, D.C.

Chapter 2

DEFINING INTERNATIONAL PUBLIC GOODS:

Conceptual Issues

Oliver Morrissey, Dirk Willem te Velde, and Adrian Hewitt

International public goods (IPGs) achieved prominence with the United Nations Development Programme's publication *Global Public Goods* (Kaul, Grunberg, and Stern 1999). That study adopted a wide-ranging definition of IPGs that encompassed a broad range of development activities. Analytically, the definition has since been narrowed by, for example, Kanbur, Sandler, and Morrison (1999). Operationally, the World Bank (2001) has further distinguished between core and complementary activities associated with the provision of IPGs (see also chapter 1 in this volume). The essential point here is that IPGs provide widely available benefits, and providing these benefits is the core activity. However, helping people or countries to actually avail themselves of the public goods (to "consume" them) may also be necessary. Such enabling expenditures are complementary to the core activities.

In this chapter we attempt to pull together current thinking on an appropriate delineation of IPGs. Our goal, in part, is to provide a basis for chapter 5, which quantifies the extent to which donor aid has financed the provision of public goods. What exactly are IPGs? How can we assess whether official development assistance is succeeding in providing them? This chapter first attempts to define public goods, then classifies them according to the types of benefits they yield from the perspective of users, and finally relates these categories to sectoral expenditures that are most likely to provide benefits that have an international scope. We also discuss some implications for the financing of IPGs, in particular, the nature of cost-sharing arrangements that may be reasonable when citizens of different countries value the same public good very differently.

This chapter reaches three main conclusions:

- The definition of IPGs is not precise, but operationally useful characterizations are possible.
- IPGs are most relevant in the areas of health, the environment, knowledge, security, and possibly economic and financial governance.
- To deal with the problem of differential valuation of public goods, breaking their costs of provision into those for research, coordination, and implementation may help make the financing problem more tractable.

INTERNATIONAL PUBLIC GOODS AND EXTERNALITIES: SOME DEFINITIONS

The concept of IPGs is not as clearly defined as one would wish. A large literature is now available, and while there is broad consensus on what is at stake and on what is being discussed, the writers' nuances differ. Each of the three words—"international," "public," and "good"—can be questioned. In this section we examine these words as a prelude to reaching an operational definition. We also briefly consider the difference between the term public goods and the concept of externalities, and conclude that they have the same practical implications for the purpose of the IPG research and policy agenda.

How Public Are Public Goods?

A classic economic definition of a public, or social, good is one "which all enjoy in common in the sense that each individual's consumption of such a good leads to no subtraction from any other individual's consumption of that good" (Samuelson 1954, p. 387). This definition implies that a pure public good must exhibit two characteristics. First, it should be nonexcludable, meaning that once the good has been provided, nobody can be excluded from enjoying its benefits. Because free-riding cannot be prevented, in this context setting a market price is not effective, and hence provision of a pure public good would not be attractive to the private sector. If excludability is difficult or costly, there is a case for public provision of the good, or of a public contribution to the cost of providing the good, so that the socially optimal level of provision is attained. Second, a public good should be nonrival in consumption, which means that consumption by one person does not diminish the amount available to others. According to Kanbur, Sandler, and Morrison (1999, p. 61): "When benefits are non-rival it is inefficient to exclude anyone who derives a positive benefit, because extending consumption to more users creates benefits that cost society nothing."

In practice, goods will tend to exhibit neither characteristic completely, and will therefore be impurely public. Many goods may be quasi-public or mixed public and private, in the sense that they are either nonexcludable or nonrival, but not both (see chapter 4). Thus the degree of "publicness" refers to the extent to which people can be prevented from benefiting once the good is provided. In the case of a pure public good, nobody can be prevented from enjoying the benefits, and the benefits enjoyed by others do not reduce the amount of the benefit available to anybody else. A lighthouse is a classic example: passing ships cannot be prevented from benefiting from its presence (however, see Coase's 1990 critique of this example). While one might think of air traffic control or satellite communications as providing a similar type of benefit, there is an important difference: preventing some from benefiting is technically feasible. This possibility of exclusion means that such goods are not purely public, and they are described as club goods, because only members of the club are granted the benefits.

Public goods are undersupplied for two reasons. First, to an individual, the investment cost of provision may exceed the returns. This essentially follows from the inability to exclude potential beneficiaries from obtaining the benefits, which implies that some or all of the beneficiaries will not pay for the benefits, that is, they will free-ride. Second, even if charging for the benefits received were possible, as noted, not everyone values the public good to the same extent. Although in principle everybody benefits from public goods, some will derive more utility from the good than others. Reducing greenhouse gas emissions, for example, would appear to be a global public good, because it reduces the climatic risk associated with global warming, and this is a benefit to all. However, some may not perceive the benefit or may not rank it high among their preferences, and therefore do not derive utility. As a consequence, the design of prices to be charged is rendered extremely complex.

How International Are International Public Goods?

Does the term international mean that the benefits are completely global, in the sense that everybody on the globe benefits? In a broad sense the answer may be yes, but in a narrow sense it may be no. Almost everyone would agree that, for example, eradication of a disease such as malaria is an IPG. In principle, everybody benefits because the risk of contracting the disease is eliminated. In practice, however, the initial risk of contracting the disease is effectively zero for many people. From a practical perspective, the differences in the value placed on an IPG have implications for beneficiaries' willingness to contribute to the cost of providing the public good, because the size of the perceived benefit accruing to potential contributors influences their willingness to pay for the required investment.

Thus the spatial range over which measurable benefits are economically meaningful is different for different public goods. The spillover range to which the benefits apply can extend from the truly global to mainly the local or the community level, with international, regional, and national levels arrayed in between (see chapter 3 for a detailed discussion). We use the term international to signify that while the benefits extend well beyond national boundaries, they may not apply everywhere on the globe. A regional public good is one whose benefits accrue to the publics of neighboring nations (see chapter 6). Similarly, a national public good is one whose benefits accrue mainly to a particular country's public, while a local public good is one whose benefits are largely subnational.

The delineation of each point on the spectrum from international to local is, however, often unclear. National-level education would be considered a national public good, as the benefits accrue largely to the nation collectively; however, if educated people can migrate, does this imply cross-border effects? The answer depends on whether the individual migrant derives mainly a private benefit. If the migrant is fully compensated in the destination country, that country does not derive a public good. However, the act of migration may provide an IPG if the productivity benefits to the destination country are greater than the wages paid to the migrant.[1] In our analysis, here and in chapter 5, we find it useful to consider education as a national public good, but one that is a necessary complement to IPGs.

What Is Good about a Public Good

The final semantic issue concerns the word good. This is relatively straightforward: it means benefits that provide utility or satisfy wants. It does not mean merchandise, as in goods and services, nor should it be interpreted as normative, as in for the good of the public, even if it is. In this sense the elimination of a "public bad" (where bad means disutility), for example, disease or pollution, is a public good.

Definition

The foregoing discussion thus leads to a definition: *an international public good is a benefit providing utility that is, in principle, available to everybody throughout the globe.*

Public Goods and Externalities

While, in theory we can distinguish clearly between public goods and the concept of externalities, in practice the two concepts overlap. The essential feature of a public good is that, once provided, the same quantity is available for consumption by all individuals within the spatial range, and this single quantity is also the total amount of the good available. By contrast, in the case of a private good the total quantity available is the sum of the amounts consumed by each individual. An externality, however, does not refer to the quantity of the good available, but to the interdependence between agents. In particular, it refers to "an interdependence that occurs outside of the price mechanism" (Cullis and Jones 1992, p. 41). That is, consumption or production by one agent has effects on other agents, either as consumers or producers.

In practice, paying too much attention to the distinction between public goods and externalities may not be helpful. For example, pollution generated as part of a production process is an externality (an external bad). As pollution accumulates over time and spreads across borders, what was an externality effectively becomes an international public bad, for example, through ozone depletion or global warming. A case then emerges for contributing to providing an IPG, that is, reducing ozone depletion or greenhouse gas emissions. Standard public intervention to reduce this externality could be through taxation, which imposes a price for the disutility caused and reduces consumption, or through regulation, which creates specific restrictions on production technologies. Similarly, vaccinating somebody against a disease is a private good, but one that has an externality. Because the person is not going to catch the disease, and is therefore not going to spread it, there is an external good, the reduced risk of contagion. This external good provides a public good: the reduced risk of spreading the disease. Thus in practice one cannot distinguish precisely between the externality and the public good. However, in each case the implications for how the public good should be provided and how it should be financed is likely to vary. For instance, the best option for the pollution example may be for the polluter to pay and for the vaccination case to provide free vaccinations.

TYPES OF PUBLIC BENEFITS AND PUBLIC GOODS

Public goods, that is, goods that give rise to benefits that tend to be nonexcludable and nonrival, can be divided into three groups: those that directly provide utility, those that reduce risk, and those that enhance capacity. While we discuss each in turn, they are inter-related, and a particular public good may provide all three types of benefits.[2] If the benefit provides direct utility or reduces risk, the public good is more likely to be international, because in principle, everybody can benefit. If, however, the benefit is to enhance capacity, its spatial range is more likely to be limited. Table 2.1 classifies IPGs based on the nature of the benefits.

Several examples illustrate the direct utility provided by public goods. Reducing the environmental degradation of a common property resource, such as an ocean or a forest, improves the quality of the natural resource, for instance, through undertaking conservation activities or preserving biodiversity. The increased quality of the resource can enhance its productivity and sustainability, which generates externality benefits (capacity enhancement) that all can enjoy. Reducing poverty has a public good element in the same sense, that is, everybody can derive utility from the knowledge that poverty has been reduced. However, the public good is the knowledge that poverty has been reduced rather

Table 2.1. Classification of IPGs by Range and Types of Benefits

	Type of benefit		
Range of benefit	*Direct utility*	*Risk reduction*	*Capacity enhancement*
Global	Conserving biodiversity	Reduced climatic risk; reduced risk of financial instability	Global governance institutions; global knowledge generation
Regional	Protecting forests and lakes; peace-keeping	Reduced acid rain; lower incidence of disease	Research on arid agriculture

Source: Authors.

than the actual reduction of poverty (poverty reduction is not a public good, because increasing the incomes of poor people is both excludable and rival).

Many public goods provide a benefit that is in the form of reduced or eliminated risk, where the risk is a disutility (or, in general, a public bad). Reducing greenhouse gas emissions lowers the risk of global warming for everybody. By contrast, reducing the risk associated with the pollution or exploitation of a common property resource, such as an ocean, a lake, or a forest, is also a public good, but may have a limited spatial range (regional or national) depending on who shares the resource. For example, reducing the acid rain generated by the United Kingdom has benefits that are limited to other European countries (see chapter 3). Pollution of the oceans imposes disutility at an international level, so reduction of this pollution is an IPG. The same argument can apply to the reduction of airborne pollution.

Reducing the risk associated with a disease is of greatest benefit to those who live in areas where the disease is prevalent, and therefore tends to be a regional public good. Improving security and related issues of peacekeeping and reducing international crime are also public goods. If the reduced risk of conflict (or, more generally, of insecurity) applies globally, it is an IPG. Given the prevalence of international terrorism and the spillover of refugees, many conflicts have an international dimension. Often, however, the benefits will be regional or, on rare occasions, national.

Another set of public goods arises because the benefit is to enhance the capacity to produce goods (which may be public or private), where the enhanced capacity is a benefit available to all. It is the enhanced capacity that constitutes the public good, not necessarily the goods that may be produced as a result. Knowledge is an example. In principle, knowledge is available to all equally; however, some may be constrained in their ability to access or use the knowledge, implying the need for complementary public goods. Knowledge itself is nevertheless an IPG. Education enhances national capacity, and is therefore a national public good. Education also enhances the capacity to produce global knowledge, and is therefore an activity complementary to providing the IPG. Governance could also be included in this group of public goods, because it enhances capacity, and good governance does, in principle, provide utility to all. Institutions relating to global or regional governance contribute to global or regional public goods, although in most cases governance is a national public good.

The three different types of public goods can be inter-related and can mutually reinforce each other, for example, reducing global warming may provide benefits of all three forms. The core versus complementary distinction is relevant here. Consider some definitions (World Bank 2001, p. 133):

> Core activities aim to *produce* international public goods. These activities include global and regional programs undertaken with a transnational, or multicountry, interest in mind, as well as activities that are focused in one country but whose benefits spill over to others.
>
> Complementary activities, in turn, prepare countries to *consume* the international public goods that core activities make available—while at the same time creating valuable national public goods. Traditional country-based financial flows to support domestic policy and institutional reform and investment in infrastructure are primarily motivated by the benefits expected within the country. But these flows and the national public goods they help create may also enhance the country's ability to absorb the benefits of international public goods.

Thus core refers to the provision of the global benefit or, in other words, the production of the IPG. Complementary refers to helping in providing the good or assisting in the ability to derive utility from the presence of the public good. This is the production-consumption distinction. For example, eliminating malaria would be a core IPG. Knowledge, and the research generating such knowledge, would contribute directly to the core public good. However, individual countries would have to contribute to provision through, for example, controlling mosquitoes. Such control would be a complementary activity (which may be a public good) that is necessary to ensure provision of the core activity. Consider knowledge, whose availability is an IPG. To avail themselves of knowledge, however, people require education, therefore education is a complementary public good that facilitates consumption. Furthermore, contributing to global knowledge requires education and research, hence education is also a complementary activity that contributes to the provision (production) of the core activity.

MAPPING THE PUBLIC GOODS CLASSIFICATION INTO "SECTORS"

Having identified the types of benefits that give rise to public goods, we can identify "sectors" for public goods: the environment, health, knowledge, security and peace, and governance. Three of these sectors are largely associated with benefits derived from reducing risk (the environment, health, and security), and two are primarily associated with enhancing capacity (knowledge and governance).

All IPGs are core activities in the sense defined earlier. Core public goods may be international or national in range. For example, the provision of health and of peace are core public goods, and this applies equally at an international or a national level. If these core public goods are provided at all national levels, this provides the IPG (although additional elements such as coordination may be involved at the global level). Equally, if some countries do not provide the good nationally, this will diminish, and may even negate, provision at the global level. In this sense national public goods are complementary to IPGs. Where this complementarity is on the production side, that is, national public goods contribute to the provision of IPGs, then both can be considered core, but with a different spillover range. Where the national public good is more relevant to consumption or utilization of the IPG, then it is a complementary activity. Let us elaborate by example, considering the five categories of public goods. A summary of the discussion is provided in table 2.2, which provides a link to the categorization used in chapter 5.

- *Environment.* The public good or activity is to provide environmental quality. As most aspects of environmental management have international dimensions, this is a core IPG. The benefits accrue principally in the form of risk reduction, though a cleaner environment is also directly valued. Either way, improved environmental quality tends to have an international spillover range. For example, reducing industrial pollution around a city will improve air quality and reduce the risk of illnesses in the locality. However, the reduced emissions may contribute to reducing global pollution. Conservation or preservation activities in forests or nature reserves are basically national or local public goods, but they do provide potential utility to all, and therefore have an international dimension. Such activities may be core at a national or local level, but complementary at an international level.

- *Health.* The public good is to improve health status, and this applies at the national and international levels. The eradication of disease is the core activity for the IPG. If the disease is contagious, each afflicted country has to be able to contribute to control and reduction. This implies that it has a health service, a national public good that is a complementary activity to providing the IPG. Similarly, if a health care system exists, this facilitates consumption of the public good.

- *Knowledge.* Knowledge itself is an IPG. Core activities at the global level include international research centers, for example, the international agricultural research centers contribute both to global knowledge and to research on how to provide environmental public goods. Research centers are a core knowledge activity, but are also complementary to providing other categories of public goods. Complementary activities also include those that contribute to disseminating knowledge, such as maintaining Internet sites and global networks, such as the World Bank's Global Development Network. The provision of schools and teachers (a national public good) and access to information are complementary activities that facilitate the use of knowledge.

- *Security.* Global peace is an IPG. Activities that contribute to peace or security, such as conflict prevention, are core activities. Similarly, institutions such as the United Nations Security Council are complementary activities at an international level, while policing is complementary at a national level.

- *Governance.* Stable, good governance is a public good, both in providing utility and enhancing capacity (and potentially in reducing the risk of

Table 2.2. Examples of International and National Public Goods by Sector

Sector and scope	Core activity	Complementary activity
Environment		
International	Research to reduce emissions	Regulation and tax incentives
National	Conservation	Environmental education
Health		
International	Research to eliminate disease	Vaccine distribution system
National	Preventive health care	Health care system
Knowledge		
International	Specialized research centers	Internet infrastructure
National	Education service	Education infrastructure
Security		
International	Conflict prevention	Institutions for conflict management
National	Crime reduction	Policing
Governance		
International	Multilateral institutions	Strengthening domestic civil society
National	Good government	Civil service reform

Source: Authors.

insecurity). The core activity is establishing global institutions to coordinate the provision of, if not to directly provide, IPGs. Thus the United Nations system and the Global Environment Facility, for example, are core activities. At the national level good governance is a core activity, but providing government capacity is complementary.

Institutions that coordinate and monitor the global economy, such as the World Trade Organization, can contribute to global stability and support core activities. Such organizations monitor and enforce agreements that support the provision of IPGs (see chapter 3). Financial instability, and macroeconomic instability in general, are bad for individual countries, but do not affect all people equally. Consequently, providing financial stability in one country is not an IPG; however, stability in one country contributes to overall stability and to governance in that country, hence it is complementary.

FINANCING IMPLICATIONS FOR DEVELOPING COUNTRIES

The choice of whether or not to provide an IPG is based on cost-benefit analysis (see chapter 3 for an extensive discussion). If the benefit is worth less than the cost, globally and for each country, then the public good should not be provided. The cost-benefit calculation is typically difficult. Often the costs of provision are easier to calculate than the benefits, especially as the benefits are a future flow subject to uncertainty. A problematic feature of many IPGs is that the benefits are largely intangible. This is most evident where the benefits take the form of providing a direct utility, such as knowing that poverty has been reduced or biodiversity has been increased. Quantifying the benefits of enhanced capacity in monetary form is also difficult. In principle, the benefits of risk reduction are the most amenable to cost-benefit analysis, but in practice the calculation is imprecise and somewhat subjective.

The U.S. stance on global warming provides an example. The United States has promoted carbon sinks as a low-cost means of absorbing carbon dioxide that is cheaper than reducing emissions, although some scientific evidence suggests that this approach may be ineffective. Furthermore, the United States has argued that the extent of global warming, at least that caused by greenhouse gas emissions, is exaggerated, and that the benefit of reducing emissions is therefore exaggerated. Consequently, the U.S. cost-benefit analysis comes out against reducing emissions by the amount or in the manner proposed in the Kyoto Agreement. Other countries disagree and place greater emphasis on reducing emissions.

Interesting cases are those where the benefits exceed total costs, but not necessarily for all countries. Specifically, what if the benefit to other countries of a low-income country's contribution to providing an IPG exceed the cost of provision, but the benefits to the low-income country are less than its cost? This could be the case, for example, for African countries, where even collectively, they may not be able to afford the cost of eradicating AIDS. While the industrial countries will derive some benefit from the eradication of the disease in Africa, these benefits may well be worth less than the costs. However, if any one country fails to eradicate a contagious disease (the weakest link), then the global public good is not provided. Providing an IPG requires collective action, but some would need to contribute a relatively greater share of the costs than others. The inherent nature of IPGs—their broad range, the many actors that need to cooperate, and the difficulties of monitoring compliance—combined with the absence of powerful supranational authorities, makes supplying such public goods especially difficult (see chapter 3).

In this context, distinguishing among various cost components provides some guidelines. The first component is research, and most public goods will have a knowledge component (developing the method to provide the good), which is a core activity. This will generally be provided wherever the research effort is greatest (in terms of chapter 4's terminology, research is produced by a "best shot" technology, that is, it is best conducted on a relatively large scale in a single location or in a coordinated manner). A considerable amount of publicly funded research in the industrial countries contributes to providing IPGs. Furthermore, considerable funding for international research centers comes from governments and foundations in the rich countries, that is, those with the greatest ability to pay.

The second cost component is coordination, which includes (a) setting priorities and reviewing how to deliver the core activity, (b) mobilizing resources and allocating funding for provision, and (c) monitoring contributions to provision. This requires funding for agencies or global institutions. Coordination of provision (setting priorities and monitoring what various actors do) is not the same as coordinating funding and need not be done by the same agency. The World Bank already acts as a coordinator of funding (World Bank 2001): trust funds administered by the World Bank contribute about US$0.8 billion annually to finance IPGs. However, a specialist agency, or even just an advisory committee, that consists of experts in the field should be established to set priorities and guidelines on how the core activity should be delivered. This is what has normally happened: an agency is established that has the requisite global expertise, sets priorities, and identifies the actions necessary to provide the IPG. This agency is then housed in, or offered institutional support by, an established organization that assists on the financial side of provision. As in the case of knowledge activities, the financing of global institutions reflects ability to pay, and also relates to enhancing capacity.

The case for global coordination of actions to address global problems does not imply global financing of the actions, although it may imply global financing of the coordination agencies. Thus we can distinguish between the financing of coordination and the financing of provision. For example, international agricultural research centers provide an IPG of knowledge, and contributions to their cost are at the international level. This also applies to the institution that coordinates their activities. However, using the knowledge, for example, to promote high-yield sustainable agriculture in a particular country, requires complementary activities at a national level. Agricultural support services are, in principle, private goods, although the associated externalities justify a public subsidy of provision. The individual country should, generally, finance the complementary activities, possibly with funds borrowed from donors. In practice, as discussed later, various approaches have been attempted where even the costs of complementary activities have proved onerous.

Another example of this distinction between financing the coordination of the activity and financing the actual activity to be coordinated arises in the context of reducing financial instability, which is often treated as an IPG. An international organization that monitored and regulated capital flows and that provided advice to countries on how to manage instability would be providing a public service, although excludability is possible, therefore this is more like a club good. However, if that organization provided a loan to a country to help it deal with financial instability, this money is effectively a private good to the country. Thus the coordinating agency may exhibit features of an IPG, but funds to particular countries do not. A similar argument can be applied to debt relief. Debt relief is not itself a public good, because it is excludable, and relief to one country does not provide a benefit to all. However, it may be a way to contribute to the cost of providing national public goods if the country used the savings in interest payments to finance provision of, for example, health and education services.

The third cost component is implementation costs. In general, as already implied in the foregoing discussion, this requires complementary activities, usually national public goods, and relates to actions that reduce risk or enhance capacity. For example, a cure for AIDS, the IPG, would be of little use if it were not delivered to those who needed it. More precisely, the core activity of eradicating a disease is not provided unless those suffering can avail themselves of the cure or those susceptible to it can be vaccinated.

Different approaches can be used to meet these implementation costs where the ability to pay is limited. The Global Alliance on Vaccines and Immunization addresses this problem explicitly: donors contribute to a procurement fund for vaccines and to the costs of immunization programs (and companies may donate vaccines). Public-private partnerships are only part of the solution, however. Even if the drugs for AIDS treatments were provided free to African countries, providing treatment would be expensive. As another example, in 1997

SmithKlineBeecham (now GlaxoSmithKline) launched its initiative to eradicate lymphatic filarasis (the cause of elephantiasis), providing the drug Albendazole for free. Similar free drug offers have been made in other public-private initiatives, such as against poliomyelitis. However, the drugs are only part of the cost of implementing the treatment; the support costs of the initiative to eradicate lymphatic filarasis are estimated as US$1 billion over 10 years (*The Guardian*, February 15, 2001).

CONCLUSIONS

The fundamental feature of IPGs is their nonexcludable and nonrival nature over a global spatial range. Nonexcludability is the source of coordination and financing problems, as an incentive to free-ride always exists. Nonrivalry creates problems in providing the optimal quantity of the good. Some form of cost-benefit calculation is required to determine how much of particular public goods should be provided. This chapter has sought to provide a classification of public goods and suggested links to issues of provision, and subsequent chapters address supply and financing issues.

NOTES

1. A different example may make the point more forcefully. Consider somebody from a poor country who is educated in a rich country. The individual derives a private benefit. Assume that person then works for a global research institution. The institution's contribution to global knowledge is an IPG, but the education received by the individual is a complementary activity that helps that individual contribute to the core activity of producing global knowledge. Assume, alternatively, that the person returns to the poor country and helps that country to use or access global knowledge. Again, the individual's education is a complementary activity that enables the poor country to consume the IPG. In either case, the education is complementary and is a national public good. Education itself is not an IPG, but is a complementary activity.

2. Strictly speaking, risk reduction also provides utility or eliminates a disutility, but considering it as a separate category is helpful.

REFERENCES

Coase, Ronald. 1990. *The Firm, the Market, and the Law.* Chicago: The University of Chicago Press.
Cullis, J., and P. Jones. 1992. *Public Finance and Public Choice: Analytical Perspectives.* London: McGraw-Hill.

Kanbur, R., T. Sandler, with K. Morrison. 1999. *The Future of Development Assistance: Common Pools and International Public Goods.* Policy Essay no. 25. Washington, D.C.: Overseas Development Council.

Kaul, I., I. Grunberg, and M. Stern, eds. 1999. *Global Public Goods: International Cooperation in the 21st Century.* New York and Oxford, U.K.: Oxford University Press.

Samuelson, P. 1954. "The Pure Theory of Public Expenditure." *Review of Economics and Statistics* 36(4): 387–89.

World Bank. 2001. "Effective Use of Development Finance for International Public Goods." In *Global Development Finance.* Washington, D.C.

Chapter 3

SUPPLYING INTERNATIONAL PUBLIC GOODS:

How Nations Can Cooperate

Scott Barrett

As discussed in chapter 2, public goods have two important characteristics: use by one party does not diminish the amount of the good available to others, and others cannot be excluded from enjoying a public good, even if they had no hand in its provision. In a national context, public goods provision thus raises two problems. The first is identifying the economically efficient level of provision, a problem of valuation. The second is designing policies and institutions able to supply this level of a good, a problem of incentives. These problems also frustrate the provision of international public goods (IPGs), but in an international context, the difficulties with valuation and the setting of incentives are compounded because, in the absence of a hierarchical command structure, the mechanisms for facilitating the supply of public goods are limited, and often fragile.

Consider first the problem of valuation. Economic efficiency requires that private goods be provided to the level where the willingness of the marginal consumer to pay equals the marginal cost of production. Public goods, by contrast, should be provided to the level where the aggregate marginal willingness to pay for the good equals the marginal cost of provision (Samuelson 1954). A well-functioning market will supply efficient quantities of private goods. The supply of public goods, by contrast, requires knowledge of the demand curve for the public good, but how can the state determine aggregate marginal willingness to pay? The obvious answer is for the state to ask people how much they would be willing to pay to have the good supplied, for example, how much would people be willing to pay for an AIDS vaccine? However, this approach is vulnerable to strategic manipulation. If I am asked how much I would be willing to pay for a public good, and if my answer will affect the decision to supply the good, but I will not be asked to pay my stated amount, then I have an incentive to state a high value. If, however, I know that I will be asked to pay the amount I specify, then I will have an incentive to state a low value. A major problem for the supply of both local and international public goods is getting people to reveal these values truthfully (see, for example, Fudenberg and Tirole 1991). This is a matter for cost-benefit analysis.

Now consider the design of incentive mechanisms for supply. Suppose that we know how much of the good ought to be supplied (the valuation problem has been solved), and that our problem is only to devise a system that will supply this amount efficiently. If the public good in question is knowledge, the first option is to have the state carry out research directly; examples include the National Aeronautics and Space Administration in the United States and the Meteorological Office in the United Kingdom. A second approach is for the state to subsidize knowledge production by others. Subsidies for state universities and funding by government research councils are examples.[1] A third approach is for the government to issue patents to private firms. All three approaches have advantages and disadvantages. The difficulty of monitoring effort creates a problem of moral hazard, a serious handicap for the first two approaches. Patents, by contrast, create a long-term efficiency gain by rewarding research and development (R&D) successes, but only at the expense of creating a monopoly in the short term, thereby undermining efficiency. Another problem with the patent system is that firms are unable to practice perfect price discrimination, and so will be unable to capture the full rewards of knowledge production.

Thus supplying even local public goods in the right amounts is difficult. These problems also affect the supply of IPGs, but as noted previously, the supply of IPGs is further burdened by the institutional constraint of having to supply public goods in an anarchic legal setting. This last constraint is the focus of this chapter. The chapter offers a menu of options, starting with the *setting of standards,* which can facilitate coordination, complemented possibly by the use of *trade sanctions* as an enforcement device (the "stick") and by *financial compensation* (the "carrot"). While these devices can sometimes promote cooperation, an important conclusion of this chapter is that a one-size-fits-all solution to these problems does not exist. The best remedies to international cooperation failures are likely to be highly specific to the particular public good under consideration.

INCENTIVES FOR THE SUPPLY OF LOCAL AND TRANSNATIONAL PUBLIC GOODS

Domestic government institutions are well suited to supplying local public goods; indeed, they developed and were designed largely with this purpose in mind. To take the most obvious example, a primary function of the state is to defend its citizens from foreign attack. National defense is a public good. When the state is defended for one person, it is defended for all, and no citizen can be excluded from benefiting from the defense of the nation. Defense is costly, and to pay for it a state will tax its citizens. It may also, at least in times of necessity, impose a regime of conscription. Neither of these activities is voluntary. The state insists that its citizens pay tax. If a citizen demurs, as when Henry Thoreau famously declined to pay tax to help fund the war between the United States and Mexico, the dissenter will be thrown into jail. Similarly, draft dodgers will be pursued and, when found and convicted, sentenced to a term in prison. These heavy-handed interventions are a ubiquitous feature of government. Government is different from every other institution in being imbued with the authority to coerce—a power that it must have if it is to supply local public goods.

Government can potentially help to supply local public goods using seemingly more light-handed interventions. Imagine a lake shared by just two residents. The lake is polluted, but the two shore-owning residents agree to stop polluting the lake by installing septic tanks. The parties sign a contract saying that each will install a septic tank, and the state enforces the contract. This means that, should either party not act as promised, the injured party could seek legal redress through the courts. In this case the government facilitates the voluntary provision of a public good by means of contract enforcement. The heavy hand of government is kept in reserve, and the government only intervenes if the contract is broken (of course, if the contract is well written and the threat of government intervention is credible, the contract will not be broken).

Voluntary contracts are a common feature of market exchange, and contract enforcement is an important ingredient of a well-functioning market economy. However, voluntary contracts are rarely used to facilitate the supply of local public goods. As explained later, the incentives to free-ride usually increase with the number of parties that share a public good. If 100 residents share a lake, getting more than a few dozen to agree to install septic tanks voluntarily may be difficult, even when assisted by a contract, and even if each resident would be better off if every resident installed a septic tank. Moreover, seeking a voluntary remedy may involve substantial transaction costs. For both reasons, local government is more likely to insist that every resident install a septic tank (and this, in turn, helps explain the existence of local government in the first place). In this example, provision of the public good is effected through planning and regulation, not direct provision by the state, as in the case of national defense. The intervention is nonetheless heavy handed; it is often referred to as command and control.

More decentralized approaches are sometimes used. In Sweden sulfur emissions are taxed, and in the United States sulfur emissions are traded like a commodity, but in both cases enforcement remains centralized. In Sweden individual polluters decide how much to pollute, but the state imposes the penalty (sulfur tax) for polluting. In the United States a utility can pollute as much as it likes, but it must pay a stiff fine if it pollutes more than its pollution permits allow.

International institutions are much weaker than domestic institutions. There is no world government with the authority to supply public goods directly, financed by taxing the global citizenry, or indirectly, for example, by telling individual countries how much of the public good they must supply. Nor is there an international institution capable of enforcing an agreement among countries to supply public goods. In the horizontal world of international governance, there can be no third party enforcement. While states do enter into agreements—treaties—to supply transnational public goods, such agreements must be self-enforcing. Self-enforcement is a problem, because the provision of public goods is vulnerable to free-riding behavior.

The rest of this section describes how the incentive problems can be resolved at the local level, followed by an example illustrating the differences between the provision of local and IPGs, and concludes with examining the potential for complementarity between local and IPGs.

Local Institutions for Solving Collective Action Problems

Research over the last 10 years or so has shown that free-riding at the local level is often less severe than the theory of collective action supposes, raising the hope that the same might be true at the international level. In particular, Ostrom (1990) has shown that local communities are sometimes able to overcome or short-circuit the incentives to free-ride in managing common property resources. However, the circumstances are crucial to this success, and the circumstances will be different at the international level.

First, the local community must be able to deter entry by outsiders, and for international supply problems, deterrence of this kind is infeasible by definition (when a transnational public good is supplied by one state, other countries cannot be excluded from benefiting). Public goods problems are in this sense harder to remedy than common property problems. Second, local communities are, by definition, homogeneous assemblages of people who live near one another and who have intimate connections. We may speak of the "community of nations," but nations are separated by their differences. Communities are bound together by their common heritage as well as their common interests. It is one thing for neighbors in a Swiss village to manage their communal grazing lands, but quite another for some 195 different countries to regulate the global climate. Third, even though the research shows that common property resources can be effectively managed without the strong and visible hand of government intervention, the central government may still play an important, if subtle, indirect role. Central government legally circumscribes the activities of organizations like cooperatives—for example, through antitrust laws. It assigns property rights, even if to communities rather than to individuals. And it can always intervene if local community management fails.

Indeed, even at the local level Baland and Platteau (1996) propose a co-management approach in which local communities collaborate with the state in creating and sustaining common property management regimes. This option, however, is unavailable at the international level.

To sum up, local public goods are supplied within a vertical or hierarchical system of governance. International public goods must be supplied by the horizontal or anarchic system of international relations. This difference is crucial, and means that we must use different kinds of institutions to effect the supply of regional or global public goods. It also means that that the international system may not be able to sustain a first-best (Pareto efficient) outcome. The constraint of self-enforcement may force us into a second-best situation. However, the outcome that we realize depends significantly on institutional design, which in turn depends on our ability to think strategically.

Differences between Local and International Public Goods

An excellent example of a global public good is global climate change mitigation. The benefit one country obtains from a reduction in climate change does not reduce the benefit that any other country obtains from this reduction. Moreover, a country's mitigation efforts cannot be nationalized. Other countries cannot be excluded from enjoying the benefits of mitigation, even if they did not contribute toward the mitigation. The supply of public goods is therefore vulnerable to free-riding.

To see the difference in the supply of local versus global public goods, let us contrast the U.S. sulfur trading program with the Kyoto Protocol, an agreement intended to moderate human-induced global climate change. Trading in entitlements is a central feature of both the U.S. acid rain program and the Kyoto Protocol. The primary difference is that the scarcity of sulfur permits in the United States is backed by the U.S. Congress's promise not to change the total quantity of permits available and not to renege on its promise to penalize compliance violations. Evidently the market perceives these promises to be credible, otherwise trading would not take place. The total quantity of permits available under the Kyoto Protocol depends on the extent of participation in the agreement, which is highly uncertain. Moreover, the incentive to trade depends on every potential trading country believing that other countries will comply with the agreement and not pollute more than their permit holdings entitle them to do. However, Kyoto was designed not to incorporate strong enforcement measures (compliance entailing "binding consequences" must be agreed by an amendment, and an amendment is essentially a new treaty). Even though a noncompliance penalty was agreed on during the Bonn meetings in July 2001, this penalty is unlikely to influence behavior by much, not least because it relies entirely on self-punishment.

Connections between Local and International Public Goods

Local and international public goods can be substitutes or complements for each other. Climate change adaptation, a local public good, is a partial substitute for climate change mitigation, a global public good. The development of new transportation technologies holds the promise of reducing urban pollution, a local public good, and greenhouse gas emissions, a global public good.

Local institutions may also matter for the supply of both local and global public goods. There is contrasting evidence on whether democracy promotes or harms growth. However, Barrett and Graddy (2000), in a modification to Grossman and Krueger's (1995) celebrated paper on the so-called environmental Kuznets curve, find that countries with greater civil and political freedoms supply higher levels of local environmental quality, particularly those aspects of environmental quality closely associated with human health. This suggests that democratic institutions may be more important as regards the supply of public goods than private goods (the latter are included in estimates of net national product, changes in which are counted as growth).

Do these same institutions promote the provision of global public goods? Some evidence suggests that they might (see Congleton 1992; Fredriksson and Gaston 1999; Murdoch and Sandler 1997; Murdoch, Sandler, and Sargent 1997). However, the problem with using regression analysis to make this connection is that countries' decisions to participate in an international agreement are interdependent. Consider, for example, participation in the Montreal Protocol, the subject of Congleton's analysis. As discussed later, the coupling of trade restrictions and an offer to pay compliance costs removed any disincentive undemocratic countries may have had to participate in this agreement. The vast majority of nondemocratic countries participate fully in the agreement.[2] However, overall the evidence that local public goods are more likely to be supplied in abundance by more democratic states strongly suggests that more democratic countries are also more likely to promote the supply of IPGs.

IDENTIFYING THE CORE IPG PROVISION CHALLENGES

Though the provision of IPGs is often problematic, sometimes these problems are easily overcome. Thus, for practical policymaking, it is important to delineate the types of situations in which IPGs will not be provided. This section outlines the conditions under which active international policymaking can make a difference.

Consider a situation in which the supply of a global public good is determined by collective effort (a "summation good" in the terminology of chapter 4). An example is protection of the ozone layer. The amount of protection available to every country depends on the sum of the protection levels undertaken by all countries. For simplicity, assume that supply at the level of the state is binary: the good is either supplied or it is not, that is, ozone-destroying chemicals are either prohibited or not.

What will happen in this situation depends on the benefits and costs of provision at the local level. Suppose that the benefit to country i of i's own supply exceeds the cost of supply. Then country i clearly has every incentive to supply the good unilaterally, and if the same is true for every country, a first-best outcome will be supported. Here provision is not a problem. This situation roughly characterizes protection of the ozone layer by some countries in a preliminary stage of the international cooperation effort (Barrett 1990). The main point is that supply is not a problem for every public good. Countries may have unilateral incentives to supply some IPGs.

Now suppose that the benefit to all countries of country i's supply is less than the cost of supply. If this were true for every country i, global welfare would be maximized if the good were not supplied by any country. The point here is that we may be better off without some public goods. Just as benefit-cost analysis is needed to justify country projects, it is also needed to justify the provision of global public goods. This is why valuation is important.

The Prisoners' Dilemma

The situation we will be mainly interested in is one that falls between these two extremes, that is, one in which the benefit to all countries of having country i supply the good exceeds i's cost, but one in which the benefit to i also falls short of i's cost. This is a prisoners' dilemma. The prisoners' dilemma problem poses the greatest challenge to the international system, though, as noted above, we should not be misled into thinking that every public goods problem is a prisoners' dilemma. It is important, moreover, to be specific about the conditions under which the prisoners' dilemma is a problem.

A few qualifying observations are useful here. The first two of these observations serves to mitigate the severity of the IPG supply problem, while the last aggravates the consequences of the lack of international cooperation. First, in the foregoing analysis I took the public good to be binary: it was either provided or it was not provided. Some public goods are binary, but most can be supplied along a continuum. Greenhouse gases may be abated 3.6 percent or 87.2 percent, and knowledge may be supplied in varying quantities. Often states will have an incentive to supply some amount of a public good, but not as much as would be required by full cooperation (a first best). Evidence that some amount of a transnational public good is being provided thus does not indicate that enough is being provided. Often the problem is not zero provision, but underprovision.

Second, if a transnational public good is underprovided, some states may take actions that limit the harmful consequences for welfare. If too little mitigation is undertaken to limit global climate change, states will invest more in adaptation (which is either a private good or a local public good), thereby limiting the damage caused by climate change. If an AIDS vaccine is unavailable, states will invest more in education about the disease, and people will adjust their behavior to reflect the risks they face. Welfare will be increased by these kinds of responses relative to a situation in which offsetting responses are infeasible. The damage associated with the failure to supply the transnational public good will be reduced.

Finally, however, the provision of transnational public goods has important dynamic incentive effects. If incentives to reduce greenhouse gases are absent, for example, incentives to develop new technologies capable of producing energy with fewer emissions will be stunted. In many cases the long-term consequences of public goods underprovision will be more important than the immediate consequences.

In the equilibrium to the one-shot prisoners' dilemma, every player fails to cooperate. If the game were repeated indefinitely, however, and if every player were sufficiently patient, then failure by every player to supply the public good may still be an equilibrium, but so will every other feasible outcome, including full provision (see, for example, Fudenberg and Maskin 1986). The theory of repeated games thus begs the question of whether the supply of transnational public goods really is a problem.

However, the notion of an equilibrium that underlies the folk theorems is ill-suited to international cooperation problems (Barrett 1994, 1999c). The provision of transnational public goods is a cooperative effort. Individual rationality is crucial to an equilibrium because of sovereignty: international law lays down the rules of the game, and these rules say that countries are free to participate or not in an international agreement seeking to supply a public good. However, collective rationality is also important. If a country chooses not to participate, the other countries will consider their situation collectively and not just individually. In particular, they will punish the deviant state only if doing so makes them collectively, and not just individually, better off. Collective rationality essentially requires that countries take some account of their collective interests not just when cooperation succeeds, but also when it fails. In the language of game theory, collective rationality should apply not just on the equilibrium path, but also off it.

Collective rationality gives precision to our predictions about cooperation. Under certain plausible assumptions, it yields a unique equilibrium (Barrett 1999c). It also limits cooperation. In particular, the success of international agreements will depend on the nature of the problem: the payoffs to the players, both the functional specification and the parameter values, and the number of players. Cooperation is much easier when the public good is regional. All else being equal, global public goods are the hardest to supply.

The intuition behind this result is that to deter any country from failing to supply the public good, other countries must threaten to punish a deviant for failing to supply it. However, when they punish a deviant by reducing their provision of the public good, these other countries harm themselves. This is especially bad from their collective perspective, and makes the threat to punish incredible. The larger the number of countries, the greater the cost of enforcement to the collective of all countries required to punish a deviation, and the less credible the threat to enforce.

As noted earlier, this approach leads us to a clear prediction. If we weaken the assumption of collective rationality a little, we lose some of this clarity, but we gain something else: it becomes possible for countries to negotiate different kinds of treaties (Barrett 2000). In particular, they might negotiate a narrow but deep treaty, that is, an agreement in which every signatory supplies a lot of the public good, but in which participation is thereby limited. Or they might negotiate a broad but shallow treaty, that is, a treaty in which every country participates, but where each signatory supplies only a small quantity of the public good. This approach should make us pause. It tells us that even if all countries cooperate in supplying a public good, the level of provision may be too low. Failures of collective action can be manifest in underprovision as well as in nonparticipation.

The most basic point is that sovereignty implies that sustaining a first-best outcome may not be possible every time. Global public goods are especially difficult for the international system to supply in efficient quantities. When we think about the supply of global public goods we should be thinking about what is feasible given the constraints imposed by sovereignty rather than about what is ideal.

The Weakest Link Game

Even when a situation does not resemble a prisoners' dilemma, provision of the public good is not assured. Consider, for example, the weakest link game. In this game every country must provide the public good in order for each country to gain by providing it. Essentially, the net benefits of providing the public good are nonlinear. An example is the eradication of a contagious disease (Sandler 1997 and chapter 4). For the disease to be eliminated everywhere, every state must control the disease at home. If just one state fails to play its part, the disease may continue to exist, and if it does it will pose a risk to every other state.

This kind of situation makes it seem that provision is difficult, but the reverse is actually the case. As long as the benefit to every country of eradication exceeds the cost of controlling the disease within its own borders, each country will have a strong incentive to eradicate the disease locally, provided each is assured that every other country will do the same. This is a coordination problem. For a coordination problem a treaty may be required to ensure that the required assurance is given, but enforcement will not be a problem. Recall that the problem with supplying regional and global public goods is enforcement. Where a problem requires only coordination, a first best should be attainable, even in the anarchic international system.

Unfortunately, situations of this kind are rare. Even for disease control, coordination will usually be insufficient. Many countries have strong incentives to control infectious diseases at home, even if every other country takes no such measures. Suppose that a vaccine were available. Then a local vaccination program would protect the local population from the disease, whether or not other countries vaccinated their populations. Now look at this situation from the perspective of these other countries. They benefit somewhat from the vaccination efforts of others, because these immunizations reduce the force of the disease (Anderson and May 1991), but this also means that these other countries have a reduced incentive to immunize. Indeed, this is one reason why disease is hard to control even within a country. As the prevalence of a disease falls, the risk of getting the disease falls, and people take fewer precautions. When people stop taking precautions—when they stop getting vaccinated— the population of people susceptible to the disease increases and the disease has a new population to infect.

Strategic Substitutes and Complements

In the prisoners' dilemma, game players have dominant strategies. It is in every player's interests to defect, irrespective of whether the others defect or cooperate. Usually this will not be a characteristic of public goods supply. Often what one country does depends on what others do. We have already seen this in the case of the weakest link game. Where the incentive to vaccinate decreases in line with the vaccination efforts of others, vaccination is a strategic substitute. Another example is pollution control, where the marginal benefits of control decrease in line with the level of control. As one country reduces its pollution, the marginal benefit to others of reducing their pollution falls, making abatement less attractive to these countries. This is a kind of negative feedback.

In some situations positive feedback exists. Imagine a situation where as one country reduces its pollution, the cost to other countries of reducing their pollution falls. Then abatement by one country will cause others to abate more. Suppose that a country establishes a new pollution standard, forcing development of a new technology capable of meeting the standard. Part of the cost of developing the technology, including the R&D costs and the costs of testing the new technology, will be fixed. Some of these costs, once incurred, will also be sunk. This means that after the technology has been developed, it can be offered at a reduced cost to other countries. This in turn means that other countries are more likely to establish a tighter pollution standard. Of course, the country that established the new standard in the first place may have foreseen this, and so may have had an incentive to behave strategically. That is, it may have set a standard that was too high relative to the level that could be justified from a myopic perspective, realizing that it would ultimately gain as other countries responded by adopting the technology and so reducing their pollution. In this case pollution abatement is a strategic complement.[3]

The elimination of chlorofluorocarbons (CFCs), chemicals now known to destroy stratospheric ozone, illustrates this kind of interdependence. The United States and a number of other countries—including Canada, Norway, and

Sweden—unilaterally reduced their consumption of CFCs in the mid- to late 1970s by banning their use in spray cans. Later, an international treaty was negotiated in which a much larger number of countries pledged to reduce their use of CFCs. This treaty—the Montreal Protocol on Substances that Deplete the Ozone Layer—imposed uniform obligations upon all its industrial country signatories. Many European countries could meet their obligations by doing what the United States and the other early-movers had previously done, but because these other countries had acted previously, the cost to European countries of eliminating the use of CFCs as aerosols was substantially reduced. Early action by the United States and other countries reduced the cost to late-movers of acting, making these countries more inclined to reduce their emissions in a subsequent period.

If this positive feedback were strong enough, a treaty to protect the ozone layer would not be needed. Just as price setting by a Bertrand duopoly forces prices to the competitive level, so abatement setting by countries would force provision of the public good of ozone layer protection to the full cooperative level. However, the Montreal Protocol kick-started the process of reducing emissions. As I have argued elsewhere (see Barrett, 1999b), the original parties to the 1987 treaty had strong unilateral incentives to reduce their emissions somewhat. Subsequent negotiations substantially increased the level of abatement. They also got the industrial countries to finance abatement by poorer countries. These later possibilities would not have been possible without the treaty.

STANDARDS AS COORDINATING DEVICES

Standards are important public goods. While some technical standards are proprietary, many are not. The standard of having a car's steering wheel on the left or the right is a public good. So is the standard for the height of a car's bumper. No one can be excluded from using these standards (although governments can exclude products that do not meet a particular standard), and one company's use of these standards does not diminish their availability to others. Other examples of open standards include telephone, fax, and Internet protocols that allow people in different countries to communicate. Standards are especially important for systems where software must be matched to hardware and in networks.

The significance of standards arises not only because they are themselves public goods, but also because they make possible the provision of public goods. In this section I first discuss the role of environmental emissions standards. Standards in this case are set on the outcome: the level of permissible emissions. Economists prefer such standards, because businesses can determine their most effective way of achieving the level of pollution permitted. However, in some instances, technical standards that specify the means of achieving the goal become necessary. I therefore consider the conditions under which a technical standard serves an important international function.

Emissions Standards: U.S. Standards as De Facto International Standards

In recent years, pollution standards have not specified a technology, but instead have specified allowed levels of emissions or of environmental quality. However, a pollution standard can often only be met by means of a technology, and so may indirectly lead to the development of a technology standard. An example is the standard for automobile emissions. The standard the United States adopted in the 1970s could only be met by use of a catalytic converter (indeed, adoption of the U.S. standard helped promote the development of this technology, an example of technology-forcing regulation). The converter itself may be patented, but the pollution standard is available to any country.

As it happens, the U.S. standard is becoming a global standard (see Faiz, Weaver, and Walsh 1996), and understanding why is important. One important reason is cost. The testing required to set an environmental standard is expensive. A link must be made between the level of emissions and human health, one that directly or indirectly takes account of both the cost of reducing emissions and the corresponding benefits in improved health. If the conditions in two different countries are similar enough, given that one country has invested in the setting of such a standard, it may not pay the other country to replicate the analysis. It may be better to copy the early-mover's standard. Allied to this reason is the need to develop technologies that can meet the environmental standard. As in the example of CFCs given earlier, once one country has incurred the costs of development and testing, the same technologies can be made available to other countries at a reduced cost. This effect will be further strengthened if manufacturing the technology entails economies of scale. If so, the fixed costs of production can be spread over a greater volume.

When a country like the United States adopts a standard that all cars sold in the United States must meet, foreign car makers have a strong incentive to produce to the same standard, because the U.S. market is too big for large foreign manufacturers to pass up. However, having invested in the design and retooling needed to supply the U.S. market, these foreign manufacturers can supply the same technology to their home markets—and, indeed, third parties—at a reduced cost, an effect that will again be amplified where there are economies of scale.

For automobiles, network effects reinforce these incentives to standardize. Catalytic converters only operate effectively in cars fueled by unleaded gas, so countries requiring the use of catalytic converters will at the same time require that unleaded gas be made widely available (all the more so because lead is itself a harmful pollutant). If the residents of one country travel by car into neighboring countries, the gas retailers in those countries will have an incentive to offer unleaded gas. Once enough gas stations have converted to unleaded gas, the cost to the neighboring countries of requiring catalytic converters will be reduced, as part of this cost is the associated cost of making unleaded gas available.

Another example is the setting of hygiene standards for the manufacture of drugs by the U.S. Food and Drug Administration. A foreign firm can sell drugs in the United States, but only if the Food and Drug Administration has approved its manufacturing facilities.

Clearly, if enough countries adopt a particular standard, the incentive for others to adopt the same standard can become overwhelming. When economies of scale are relatively small and where network connections are neither widespread nor dense, different standards may proliferate, but when a country as large as the United States adopts a standard and globalization reduces the barriers between countries, the incentive to adopt a uniform standard increases. Eventually, a tipping point may be reached where all countries adopt the same standard.

This discussion is relevant for several reasons. First, standardization, though itself a public good, helps determine the supply of other public goods. For example, automobile emissions are an important source of local pollution, and hence help determine the supply of a local public good: air quality. Automobile emissions are also a significant source of greenhouse gases, and standards for the fuel economy of cars will have implications for climate change policy worldwide. More radically, standardization could also hasten the replacement of the internal combustion engine with an alternative technology, such as the fuel cell or electric car, both of which require a network of stations for refueling. Second, a decentralized process of standard setting does not guarantee that the "right" standard is chosen. This is the main lesson of the famous QWERTY parable (see David 1985), and explains why countries may want to coordinate their standard setting.[4] A recent example is the Agreement Concerning the Establishing of Global Technical Regulations for Wheeled Vehicles, which came into force in August 2000, and which Canada, Japan, Russia, the United States, and the European Union have already ratified. Third, countries may have incentives to be too slow to change (excess inertia) or too fast (excess momentum) (see Farrell and Saloner 1985). Finally, it may be possible for countries to behave strategically, that is, to create a standard for the purpose of supplying a public good. The standard in this case is strategic, because it is only chosen to overcome incentives to free-ride (it turns a prisoners' dilemma into a coordination game).

Technology Standardization

Mitchell (1994) describes how the attempt to regulate deliberate discharges of oil into the sea by oil tankers initially failed, but later succeeded. What changed was the focus of the regulators' attention. Initially they established emission standards for the release of oil at sea. In contrast to the automobile case, this approach did not create any incentives for technology standardization. Later the regulators proposed setting technical standards directly, which dramatically altered the attitude toward cooperation.

The main problem with the emissions standards approach was that a tanker's actions could not be monitored and compliance with a standard could not be verified. Port inspections of cargo tanks were prohibited by international law because of the intrusion on sovereignty. Tanker activities could be observed from the air, but aerial photographs of a tanker in the middle of an oil slick were not accepted as legal evidence of a violation. Enforcement was another problem. Even if noncompliance were observed, only flag states could prosecute a violation. They had little incentive to do so.

The technical standards proposed later required that new tankers be fitted with segregated ballast tanks. One of the reasons for the release of oil at sea was the need to fill oil cargo tanks with water for ballast on the return journey.

With segregated tanks oil and water would not mix. The operators of ships fitted with segregated tanks had no incentive to dump their oil at sea, even if they could do so without being detected. Moreover, verification required only a quick inspection of the tanker's construction. The new agreement also allowed a ship to be detained, but even without this authority a coastal state could easily ban a ship from entering its ports if it failed to meet the required standard. Moreover, it could notify other coastal states sharing similar concerns about the ship's violation.

Mitchell argues that these incentives for compliance explain why, in contrast to its predecessors, the revised International Convention for the Prevention of Pollution from Ships (the MARPOL agreement) entered into force and reduced the practice of ocean dumping. I agree with his assessment, but believe that tanker operators may have had an additional motivation.

Tanker transport operates like a network. Tankers must be compatible with port facilities. To take an obvious example, tankers can only enter ports that are deep enough to accommodate them. Segregated ballast tanks are not a technical requirement in the same way that a ship's draft can be, but if segregated ballast tanks were required by regulation, and if ships not fitted with them could be barred from entering a port, then the regulatory standard would act like a technical standard.

Consider the problem from the perspective of the tanker operator. The value of a tanker depends on the number of ports it is able to enter (as well as the identities of these ports). If few states require segregated ballast tanks, it may not pay tanker operators to adopt the standard, at least not on all their new ships. By contrast, if most of the important oil importing and/or oil exporting states require segregated ballast tanks, then most tanker operators will prefer to adopt the segregated ballast tank standard.

Now consider this situation from the perspective of the coastal states. It may not pay a state to require segregated ballast tanks when no other country does so for the simple reason that most operators may stop making deliveries to this state, pushing up the cost of oil in this market. However, if most other states require segregated ballast tanks, then for an additional coastal state to require them will be relatively inexpensive. Probably most ships entering this country's waters will already be fitted with them.

Mitchell does not discuss these network effects, but he argues that if the United States had acted unilaterally by requiring that tankers be fitted with segregated ballast tanks—and the United States did threaten to do so—then operators would probably have modified their tankers to serve this large market only. Provided enough countries required the segregated ballast tank standard, however, then it would have been irresistible for most other states to follow. It happens that MARPOL would only come into force if ratified by enough countries to make up at least half the gross tonnage of the world's merchant shipping fleet. If my reasoning is right, then this minimum participation level indicates the tipping point for this agreement. Once this minimum was reached and the agreement entered into law, it would have paid most other states to jump on the bandwagon. This is exactly what happened. As of July 31, 2000, participation in this treaty included about 94 percent of world tonnage.

Even though MARPOL is a success, it is only an imperfect remedy. Segregated ballast tanks do not prevent the release of all oil, and the technical standard did not allow any flexibility. Had the emission standards been enforced, tanker operators may have chosen alternative ways to meet them. Economists normally favor emission standards over technology standards precisely for this reason. However, this presumes that countries have the regulatory wherewithal to monitor and enforce compliance. As regards IPGs, this capacity is often lacking.

One of the important lessons of this case is that as regards regional and global public goods, separating means from ends is not possible, or even desirable. The ends of reducing oil pollution at sea were more effectively achieved by the setting of technical standards. The technical standards approach cast the oil pollution problem as a coordination game, not a cooperation game requiring strong enforcement. However, this approach will not always be desirable, and may not even be feasible.

USING TRADE LINKAGES TO ACHIEVE COORDINATION

The reason why cooperation is limited within the foregoing framework is that when cooperating countries punish deviants, they harm themselves in the process. In a model of reciprocity, the only way that a deviant can be punished is if the cooperating countries lower their supply of the public good. Thus a threat to punish severely is unlikely to be credible. Why not punish by some other means? The obvious alternative is to impose trade restrictions; however, trade restrictions are not an easy fix.

International trade is already linked to many public goods problems. In the case of global climate change, for example, cooperation by some countries to supply mitigation may only shift pollution to other countries. In lowering pollution at home, cooperating countries essentially require that their own industries substitute away from polluting materials, and this substitution will be costly. As a consequence, comparative advantage in the greenhouse gas-intensive industries will shift toward countries that do not regulate these emissions. As a consequence of this shift in output, pollution emissions may rise in these countries. This so-called trade leakage problem exacerbates the free-riding problem. It makes unilateral or multilateral attempts at cooperation even less likely to succeed.

This concern about leakage is often voiced as a concern about a loss in competitiveness. Normally, we would not worry about such losses; production shifts are necessary for improving efficiency. However, in this case we may have reason to worry. The shift in production associated with a reduction in emissions by a block of countries may prevent these countries from realizing a welfare superior outcome.

Border tax adjustments are an obvious remedy for this problem. Suppose, for example, that a carbon tax were imposed at home. Then trade leakage could be neutralized by imposing a tariff on imports and by giving a rebate on exports. The problem is that these adjustments would need to be applied to finished goods, not just energy inputs. How could you determine the carbon dioxide emitted in the manufacture of a bottle of wine or a computer? Not only would this be a colossal task, but one that would be prone to abuse by protectionists.

There is another way to neutralize leakage. Leakage can only be a problem if participation in an agreement is less than full. If free-riding could be deterred, leakage would be stopped. We can learn more from the example of the Montreal Protocol. This agreement includes a trade restriction to be imposed by parties against nonparties in relation to CFCs and products containing CFCs.

To see why trade restrictions can promote participation, suppose that an agreement is negotiated that imposes the foregoing restriction. If just two countries participate in the agreement, they will be doubly harmed. On top of incurring substantial abatement costs, they would be unable to trade with all the other countries in these goods. It is unlikely that any country would want to participate in an agreement restricting trade with nonparties when few others participate.

Now suppose that participation is nearly full. Even though nonparties can free-ride on the public good provision by parties, they will suffer by not being able to trade with most other countries in the listed goods. If the loss is substantial enough, it will pay every country to participate if enough other countries participate. Note that the participation decision is not a dominant strategy, and that the treaty has transformed the cooperation dilemma into a coordination game. What we have here is another tipping situation (Barrett 1997).

However, we must be sure that this kind of punishment mechanism for free-riding is credible. We therefore need to ask whether if a country fails to cooperate, will it really be in the collective interests of the cooperating countries to restrict trade with this country? The answer is not obvious, because the trade restriction will normally harm the countries that impose it as well as the deviant. However, if leakage is severe enough, then the trade restriction will be credible. The reason is that if a country has chosen not to participate, production could relocate to this country, causing global emissions to rise. The trade restriction would neutralize this relocation, even if it did nothing to change this country's decision to participate. Ironically, leakage actually makes punishing noncooperation credible (Barrett 1999a).

Understanding that it is only essential that the threat to punish be credible is important. If it is credible, then it need never be carried out. In other words, the public good can be supplied without actually restricting trade.

Concluding that the same approach can be used to enforce participation in a climate change agreement like the Kyoto Protocol is tempting. However, a comparable system of trade restrictions in this case would need to be applied to every traded good, and this is unlikely to be credible. The Montreal Protocol allows parties to restrict trade with nonparties in products made using CFCs, but this provision was never implemented, because it was found to be infeasible. Fortunately, in the case of the Montreal Protocol it was also unnecessary. In the case of carbon dioxide emissions, however, this is precisely the kind of trade measure that would be needed.

FINANCING MECHANISMS TO ACHIEVE COORDINATION

What role do financial transfers play in the supply of transnational public goods? It is best to think of this question from two different perspectives: financing as a means of redistribution and financing as a device for strategy. An important current policy issue is the financing of vaccines, which are a salient international public good. I consider each of these topics in turn.

Using Financial Transfers to Redistribute Gains

If countries are asymmetric in terms of the benefits from the public goods, then financial transfers may be needed to ensure that every country benefits from participating in a treaty, compared with the alternative of not having a treaty at all. Mäler (1989), for example, has shown that the full cooperative outcome for the European acid rain game would make the United Kingdom worse off compared with the noncooperative outcome. To get the United Kingdom to join, the countries that benefit most from acid rain controls would have to compensate it for the costs of undertaking extensive abatement.

In reality, things are not so simple. It is not obvious that the noncooperative outcome is the most compelling alternative to full cooperation. The noncooperative outcome assumes that the United Kingdom has the legal right to pollute as it pleases. International law, however, says that states also have a responsibility not to harm others. Unfortunately, customary law does not provide a clear allocation of rights. It tells us that the United Kingdom cannot pollute as it pleases, but it does not tell us how much it can pollute. This is something that must be negotiated. This is a very different world from the one imagined by Coase (1960), and cannot be relied upon to yield an efficient outcome. In a negotiation in which rights cannot be assigned by a third party (a central government in Coase's article), the downwind countries are at a disadvantage because they are eager for a quick resolution. The upwind countries, by contrast, benefit from delay.

In the acid rain example, side payments have never been paid, at least not between the countries of Western Europe. This hints that the system of treaties governing long-range air pollution in Europe has probably improved little on the noncooperative outcome (see, for example, Murdoch, Sandler, and Sargent 1997). However, in other instances side payments have been paid. An important example in Western Europe is the Rhine Chlorides Agreement, whereby both upstream and downstream countries paid France to reduce salt emissions at a potash mine. However, this agreement was hardly a paragon of success: the emission reductions were delayed, a less effective control technology was eventually adopted, and economic circumstances eventually favored closure of the mine anyway. In both the acid rain and Rhine agreements, negotiations seemed only to steer countries away from a situation in which nothing was done to one in which only noncooperation was supported.

Part of the problem is that it is not enough for financial transfers to make every country better off compared with the outcome in which there is no agreement. Instead, every country must be better off being a signatory than a nonsignatory. The point is that if one country chooses not to participate, the alternative is not noncooperation but partial cooperation.

Side payments of the kind discussed here do not materially assist cooperation, because they cannot fundamentally alter the free-riding problem (Barrett forthcoming). Intuitively, money transfers are a zero sum game. For every signatory that gains, at least one other signatory must lose. Because participation in a treaty is voluntary (this is the most important expression of sovereignty), the loser can withdraw or not sign the agreement in the first place.

Financing as Strategy

Can financial transfers help sustain cooperation? Carraro and Siniscalco (1993) show that they can under some circumstances. Suppose that signatories to a treaty can commit to being signatories, then these countries have an incentive to pay other countries to join, and in this way provision of the public good can be increased.

The problem here is that countries cannot commit to being signatories. As noted earlier, international law allows countries to participate in international agreements or not as they please. Moreover, and as if to reaffirm this right, every treaty I have looked at contains an article specifying the circumstances under which withdrawals may take place (typically a period of advance notice is specified).

However, Carraro and Siniscalco's analysis is based on the assumption that countries are symmetric. As noted previously, some international agreements do incorporate financial transfers, but in all these cases countries are highly asymmetric. For example, in the Rhine Chlorides Agreement, reducing emissions at one location (France) was cost-effective. The problem was how to share the total cost. The cost-sharing formula for this treaty recognized that some countries were upstream of the pollution (France, Germany, and Switzerland), and that just one was downstream (the Netherlands).

I have shown that if countries are strongly asymmetric, then financial transfers can sustain more cooperation (Barrett forthcoming). In particular, I consider a situation in which some countries (low-benefit countries) would never be better off supplying a public good, either on their own or as part of a collective effort. However, I also suppose that there are high-benefit countries that would cooperate, fully or partially. They would also, however, be willing to pay the low-benefit countries to supply the public good. Moreover, the low-benefit countries would be willing to supply the good if compensated enough.

Strong asymmetry essentially allows the rules of the game to be rewritten. The cooperation problem changes from one in which the high-benefit countries try to cooperate to provide the public good directly to one in which the high-benefit countries try to cooperate to pay the low-benefit countries to supply the public good. Compared with the game without financial transfers, I show that, in equilibrium, the number of high-benefit signatories increases and every low-benefit country also joins. The number of high-benefit signatories increases, because contributing to the public good fund essentially ratchets up the cooperation problem. The high-benefit countries make a take-it-or-leave-it offer to the low-benefit countries, with each such country getting the minimum payment needed to make its accession individually rational. This offer is always accepted.

Consistent with the previous section, side payments alone do not assist cooperation, but only change the identities of the signatories. However, strong asymmetry means that the low-benefit countries are committed to being nonsignatories to an agreement not offering side payments. This commitment is different from the kind Carraro and Sinsicalco assumed. The low-benefit countries do not choose to be committed; they simply are committed. Schelling (1960) has emphasized the significance of this distinction.

This model helps us to understand perhaps the most important example of global public goods finance: the financial mechanism of the Montreal Protocol. In this model the Montreal Fund emerges as an equilibrium. The rich countries offer the poor countries a transfer equal to the incremental costs of their compliance, an offer that every poor country accepts.

It may seem unfair that the rich should only compensate for incremental costs. After all, this implies that the rich countries will extract the entire surplus from this positive sum game. However, the offer to compensate for incremental costs may actually yield every poor country a sizable share of the total surplus. The offer to compensate for incremental costs applies to individual countries, that is, the offer makes individual countries indifferent between joining and not joining, given the participation level. However, because the offer of compensation is made to every poor country, the participation level will rise. As long as every poor country gets a positive environmental gain from protection of the ozone layer, each will gain a positive surplus in total. Indeed, in the example given in Barrett (forthcoming), the offer of side payments actually improves the welfare of the low-benefit countries more than that of the high-benefit countries.

While side payments emerge as an equilibrium in this game, we only get to this situation after recognizing that the rules of the game can be changed by strong asymmetry. On their own, side payments make little difference, but if the players recognize that the low-benefit countries are essentially committed to remaining outside the agreement, then strategy can transform the game, and side payments must then be used to effect the transformation. The lesson is not that negotiators should use side payments when there is asymmetry, but that they should think how the game can be restructured to support greater cooperation. The usual view is that treaty negotiators simply need to find some kind of formula acceptable to a large enough number of countries. The view expressed here is different. Negotiators need to think strategically about how they can restructure their game.

Financing Vaccine Development

A number of recent proposals have been aimed at promoting vaccine development, including the Clinton administration's budget proposal for US$1 billion in tax credits for vaccine sales and the World Bank's proposed US$1 billion vaccine purchase fund. Both these proposals emphasize vaccines of particular benefit to poor countries.

Such interventions may be needed for a number of reasons. The first is that the poor countries' willingness to pay is too low to justify substantial investments by private drug companies. In other words, these funds can be seen as supplying a special kind of development assistance. A second reason is that property rights to such innovations can be insecure; designing around a patent is often easy. Finally, once a vaccine is available and the costs of R&D have been sunk, governments have an incentive to negotiate price reductions. Recall the point made earlier that patents create a short-term monopoly. This allows drug companies to charge a price well above marginal production costs. Many governments negotiate price reductions from drug companies, and this helps explain why drugs prices today are much lower in Canada and Mexico than in the United States. The difficulty is that if the United States also lowered prices in this way—and U.S. politicians will be under increasing pressure to force drug companies to do so—drug companies will have less of an incentive to innovate. Another recent reminder of this problem is the announcement by South Africa that it may require patent holders for AIDS drugs to license their patents to generic drugs manufacturers. Drug companies view this as a kind of expropriation. It essentially strips patent holders of their property rights. One can sympathize with a government wanting to alleviate the suffering of its population, but the public policy issue is not whether the surplus of an innovation should go to the drug companies or to AIDS sufferers. The public policy issue is whether the current beneficiaries of the available therapeutic drugs should gain at the expense of future beneficiaries of new drug discoveries.

As noted earlier, governments can help promote vaccine development in many ways, including direct R&D by government laboratories and grants to university researchers. However, provision by these means faces a moral hazard problem. One attraction of the vaccine purchase fund is that it pays only for research successes, not research inputs. However, the purchase fund simply shifts the moral hazard problem. The problem with "push" programs is to create incentives to carry out the promised R&D. The problem with "pull" programs is to create incentives to pay the promised amounts. If government promises were inherently more credible, the idea would have some appeal, but there is no evidence that governments can easily commit themselves in the manner suggested. If governments cannot be trusted to let firms set prices or to honor property rights, why should they be trusted to pay a high price for a vaccine after it has been developed?

Let me comment by way of a historical example. One of the great scientific challenges of the 18th century was to solve the longitude problem (see Sobel 1995). Accurate navigation—essential to both communications and trade—depends on having coordinates for both latitude and longitude. The latitude problem was solved long ago, but the measurement of longitude eluded science. To spur innovation the British Parliament announced that it would award a prize to anyone who could convince a panel of experts set up by the Royal Academy that the longitude problem had been solved. A number of people tried to solve the problem, but the first to succeed was the master craftsman

John Harrison. He invented a clock that was, for its day, astonishingly accurate. This was enough to determine longitude accurately. However, Harrison was only awarded the prize after the king intervened and ordered Parliament to pay the money. The panel of experts proved difficult to convince, and they were in any event prejudiced in favor of an intellectual solution as opposed to a practical one. This highlights another potential problem: establishing criteria for determining tolerance levels for a vaccine.

Here I would like to concentrate on a proposal put forward by Kremer (2000a,b), in which he suggests the creation of a fund for vaccines that could, by assuring a minimum purchase of the vaccine, create an incentive to invest in the necessary research efforts. How would the fund's coffers be filled? If vaccine development were a "best shot" problem, that is, if the research were best conducted in a centralized manner to take advantage of economies of scale (see chapter 4), this would not be an issue. Presumably the British were willing to pay enough to solve the longitude problem that no other country had to add to the prize. Similarly, a country like the United States would benefit enough from the development of some vaccines that international cooperation would not be needed. While the vaccines that the proposed purchase funds are intended to promote specifically benefit poorer countries, they would also have global benefits. The main point is that funding vaccine R&D is a global public good. It helps poorer countries directly, and thus every rich country indirectly, and it helps control infectious diseases and could potentially hasten their eradication.

Kremer (2000b) calculates that donor contributions of about US$750 million per year would be required to create incentives for R&D into vaccines for AIDS, malaria, and tuberculosis. Put differently, he calculates that the net present value of purchase and delivery costs over a 10-year period would be about US$3.5 billion for malaria, US$6.8 billion for tuberculosis, and US$4.3 billion for HIV. These numbers are bigger than the amounts already pledged by the United States and the World Bank, but they are relatively small. The costs per disability-adjusted life year are low. These figures are favorable for international cooperation, but more research would be needed to develop funding mechanisms that would make provision of the required funding self-enforcing.

But would this be sufficient? A safe, cheap, and effective vaccine for measles has been available since the late 1960s, yet measles remains a major killer of children in poor countries. A number of reasons account for this. One is that children in poor countries often become infected at an earlier age than in rich countries: before a vaccine is administered, but after the immunity inherited from the mother has worn off. However, this only begs the question of why more research is not being devoted to developing a vaccine more appropriate to the conditions prevailing in developing countries. Moreover, being in possession of a vaccine seems not to be a sufficient condition for safeguarding public health (see discussion in chapters 1 and 2 on the importance of complementary domestic public goods).

CONCLUSIONS

The main policy conclusions of this chapter are as follows:

- Public goods are important determinants of the material standard of living and of well-being more generally. They are therefore important to development and the goal of alleviating poverty.
- Public goods may be local, regional, or global. Traditional development assistance has helped supply local public goods like roads. It has done less to supply regional or global public goods, although as chapters 1, 5, and 6 discuss, more resources have been going to such IPGs. For example, the World Bank has played an important role as a partner both in trying to eradicate river blindness (a regional public good) and in protecting the ozone layer (a global public good).
- Supply of public goods almost invariably requires intervention by government. Indeed, government exists partly, if not largely, for the purpose of supplying public goods. For the development institutions to promote the supply of local public goods is relatively easy. To do so, they need only make arrangements with the national government (in association, perhaps, with local governments and community groups), a situation the development institutions are now comfortable with.
- Regional and global public goods cannot usually be supplied by national governments acting unilaterally. Cooperation will usually be needed.
- Cooperation in the supply of regional and global public goods is usually expressed in an international treaty of some kind supported by a variety of institutions such as a treaty secretariat.
- Effective treaty design and the development of supporting institutions require a different kind of approach from country-based approaches to

development assistance. In contrast to the supply of local public goods, a country's interest in effecting the supply of regional and global public goods will depend on what other countries are doing. The approach to the supply of such public goods must take account of this strategic interdependence.

- The nature of this interdependence varies from problem to problem. As a first step, policymakers must correctly assess the strategic aspects of the particular problem they hope to address.

    – Some public goods need only be supplied by one country, and such a country may have an incentive to supply the good unilaterally. Examples include the disease surveillance provided by the U.S. Centers for Disease Control and the efforts by the National Aeronautics Space Administration to monitor small objects in space that might conceivably collide with the earth.

    – Some public goods need to be supplied by many countries, but incentives exist for each country to supply some amount of the good, irrespective of whether other countries also supply the good. An example is the first stage of cuts in the production and consumption of ozone destroying substances achieved by industrial countries in the original Montreal Protocol.

    – Some public goods would yield an aggregate benefit that is less than the aggregate cost of supply. These goods should not be supplied. Just because a public good exists does not mean that it should be supplied. Benefit-cost analysis is as important to the supply of regional and global public goods as it is to the more routine kinds of project appraisal.

    – Some public goods, including the setting of technology standards, require multilateral coordination and no enforcement.

    – Regional public goods are easier to supply than global public goods. All else being equal, the incentives to free-ride increase with the number of countries that must supply a public good.

    – The greatest incentive problems arise in the supply of global public goods for which the efficient provision level far exceeds the amounts that individual countries will supply unilaterally. These are prisoners'-dilemma-like problems. An example would be the more extensive cuts in the production and consumption of ozone destroying chemicals achieved by amendments and adjustments to the 1987 Montreal Protocol.

- The alternative to supplying a public good is often not the status quo. Failure to supply a public good will create incentives for countries to take remedial or other actions. For example, if a disease is not eradicated, individual countries may nonetheless vaccinate their own populations. This kind of response is double-edged. On the one hand, it makes countries better off than in a situation in which such actions are not undertaken. On the other hand, it makes supply of the global public good relatively less attractive to those countries that can take such remedial or defensive actions.

- In a situation of strategic interdependence, policymakers should be aware of both negative and positive feedbacks. In some cases, as one country increases its supply of the public good, others have an incentive to reduce their supply. In different cases, others will have an incentive to increase their supply. These reactions need to be taken into account both in carrying out benefit-cost analysis and in designing institutions intended to facilitate the supply of regional and global public goods. For example, where a positive feedback is coupled with a threshold effect, a tipping point may exist, and the aim of policy may simply be to push the system over this threshold.

- Countries are interdependent not only in public goods provision, but also in trade. If public goods provision changes market prices, then it may also affect public goods provision through the trade mechanism. For example, if one country reduces its emissions of a pollutant, comparative advantage in the manufacture of this good may shift to other countries that do not take the same measures. This is called trade leakage.

- Different policy instruments may promote different kinds of strategic reactions. If one or a few countries establish an emissions standard, others may not follow (they may even increase their emissions, if for no other reason than trade leakage). However, if one or a few countries establish a technology standard that would also reduce emissions, then other countries may have incentives to adopt the same standards. This is especially likely if adoption of the technology entails strong network externalities.

- In prisoners'-dilemma-like problems, free-riding can be hard to deter. The basic reason is that the punishments that may be needed to deter countries from not cooperating will usually harm the countries that impose the punishments as well as those on the receiving end, that is, the punishments needed to deter free-riding may not be credible. As a consequence, either participation in a treaty seeking to supply a public good will be limited or the level of provision will be low. Often, sustaining a first-best outcome will not be possible. Policymakers should focus on sustainable rather than ideal provision levels.

- An exception that proves this rule about the difficulty of deterring free-riding is the Montreal Protocol, which was able to deter free-riding by threatening to impose trade restrictions between parties and nonparties. This threat seems to have deterred nonparticipation and helped increase the extent of ozone layer protection. However, the circumstances that made this possible are special. Trade restrictions are not an easy or a general remedy for the free-rider problem. Different problems will require different policy measures.

- Carrots, or side payments, may also be needed where countries are asymmetric, as is the case for global public goods. Side payments help by widening the zone of agreement. They may also ratchet up the cooperation problem. For example, in the Montreal Protocol the cooperation problem shifted from being one of getting the industrial countries to reduce their emissions to getting these countries to put up the money needed to compensate developing countries for the cost of reducing their emissions. In this treaty, side payments are used strategically.

- In general, a combination of carrots and sticks will facilitate the provision of regional and global public goods. Carrots will widen participation and ensure that all countries gain by having the agreement. Sticks will ensure that countries participate and comply. Note that carrots, when needed, will have to be paid, whereas sticks, if credible, will never actually have to be implemented. It is the deterrent effect of sticks that is important.

- Institutional connections may exist between the local level and the regional and global levels. Countries with greater civil and political freedoms may be more inclined to provide local public goods and to participate in efforts to supply regional and global public goods. At the same time, participation in regional and global efforts may strengthen a government's hand in providing local public goods.

The essential point of this chapter is that the provision of regional and global public goods requires a different kind of thinking. It requires that we think strategically.

NOTES

1. Subsidization may also take the form of so-called public-private partnerships. An example is the Medicines for Malaria initiative (Ferroni 2000), where the idea is to combine public sector funding for basic research in antimalarial drugs with private sector commitments for drug development and commercialization.

2. Congleton's (1992) analysis, which shows that more democratic countries were more likely to participate, was conducted before the Montreal Protocol was in an equilibrium situation.

3. For an analysis of strategic substitutes and complements see Bulow, Geanakoplos, and Klemperer (1985). For a discussion of how pollution control can be a kind of strategic complement see Heal (1999).

4. QWERTY refers to the arrangement of keys on a computer keyboard. Early typewriters were prone to jamming if the typist was too quick. The QWERTY arrangement was invented to slow the typist down, and thus to avoid jamming. Though the arrangement may have made sense for an earlier technology, jamming is no longer a problem, yet we retain the QWERTY arrangement. Some evidence indicates that an alternative arrangement of the keys would be faster using modern computers. Given the large installed base of QWERTY boards, however, switching to a different arrangement may not make sense, even though we might all be better off if we all switched together. Note that some controversy exists as to whether there really is a superior arrangement to QWERTY, one for which the benefit of switching exceeds the cost. However, whether true or not, the story conveys a powerful message.

REFERENCES

The word processed described informally produced works that may not be commonly available through libraries.

Anderson, R. M., and R. M. May. 1991. *Infectious Diseases of Humans: Dynamics and Control.* Oxford, U.K.: Oxford University Press.

Baland, J.-M., and J.-P. Platteau. 1996. *Halting Degradation of Natural Resources: Is There a Role for Rural Communities?* Oxford, U.K.: Clarendon Press.

Barrett, S. 1990. "The Problem of Global Environmental Protection." *Oxford Review of Economic Policy* 6(1): 68–79.

———. 1994. "Self-Enforcing International Environmental Agreements." *Oxford Economic Papers* 46: 878–94.

———. 1997. "The Strategy of Trade Sanctions in International Environmental Agreements." *Resource and Energy Economics* 19: 345–61.

———. 1999a. "The Credibility of Trade Sanctions in International Environmental Agreements." In P. Fredriksson, ed., *Trade, Global Policy, and the Environment.* Discussion Paper no. 402. Washington, D.C.: World Bank.

———. 1999b. "Montreal Versus Kyoto: International Cooperation and the Global Environment." In I. Kaul, I. Grunberg, and M. A. Stern, eds., *Global Public Goods: International Cooperation in the 21st Century.* New York: Oxford University Press.

———. 1999c. "A Theory of Full International Cooperation." *Journal of Theoretical Politics* 11(4): 519–41.

———. 2000. "Consensus Treaties." Paul H. Nitze School of Advanced International Studies, Johns Hopkins University, Baltimore, Maryland. Processed.

———. Forthcoming. "International Cooperation for Sale." *European Economic Review.*

Barrett, S., and K. Graddy. 2000. "Freedom, Growth, and the Environment." *Environment and Development Economics* 5: 433–56.

Bulow, J., J. Geanakoplos, and P. Klemperer. 1985. "Multimarket Oligopoly: Strategic Substitutes and Complements." *Journal of Political Economy* 93: 488–511.

Carraro, C., and D. Siniscalco. 1993. "Strategies for the International Protection of the Environment." *Journal of Public Economics* 52: 309–28.

Coase, R. H. 1960. "The Problem of Social Cost." *Journal of Law and Economics* 3: 1–44.

Congleton, R. 1992. "Political Institutions and Pollution Control." *Review of Economics and Statistics* 74: 412–21.

David, P. 1985. "Clio and the Economics of QWERTY." *American Economic Review* 75(2): 332–37.

Faiz, A., C. S. Weaver, and M. P. Walsh. 1996. *Air Pollution from Motor Vehicles: Standards and Technologies for Controlling Emissions.* Washington, D.C.: World Bank.

Farrell, J., and G. Saloner. 1985. "Standardization, Compatibility, and Innovation." *Rand Journal of Economics* 16: 70–83.

Ferroni, M. 2000. "Reforming Foreign Aid: The Role of International Public Goods." Annual Review of Development Effectiveness 1999. Working Paper Series no. 1. World Bank, Washington, D.C.

Fredriksson, P. G., and N. Gaston. 1999. "The Importance of Trade for the Ratification of the 1992 Climate Change Convention." In P. Fredriksson, ed., *Trade, Global Policy, and the Environment.* Discussion Paper no. 402. Washington, D.C.: World Bank.

Fudenberg, D., and E. Maskin. 1986. "The Folk Theorem in Repeated Games with Discounting or with Incomplete Information." *Econometrica* 54: 533–56.

Fudenberg, D., and J. Tirole. 1991. *Game Theory.* Cambridge, Massachusetts: MIT Press.

Grossman, G. M., and A. B. Krueger. 1995. "Economic Growth and the Environment." *Quarterly Journal of Economics* 110: 353–77.

Heal, G. M. 1999. "New Strategies for the Provision of Global Public Goods: Learning from International Environmental Challenges." In I. Kaul, I. Grunberg, and M. A. Stern, eds., *Global Public Goods: International Cooperation in the 21st Century.* New York: Oxford University Press.

Kremer, M. 2000a. "Creating Markets for New Vaccines Part I: Rationale." Harvard University, Cambridge, Massachusetts. Processed.

———. 2000b. "Creating Markets for New Vaccines Part II: Design Issues." Harvard University, Cambridge, Massachusetts. Processed.

Mäler, K.-G. 1989. "The Acid Rain Game." In H. Folmer and E. van Ierland, eds., *Valuation Methods and Policy Making in Environmental Economics.* Amsterdam: Elsevier.

Mitchell, R. B. 1994. *International Oil Pollution at Sea.* Cambridge, Massachusetts: MIT Press.

Murdoch, J. C., and T. Sandler. 1997. "The Voluntary Provision of a Pure Public Good: The Case of Reduced CFC Emissions and the Montreal Protocol." *Journal of Public Economics* 63: 331–49.

Murdoch, J. C., T. Sandler, and K. Sargent. 1997. "A Tale of Two Collectives: Sulphur Versus Nitrogen Oxides Emission Reduction in Europe." *Economica* 64: 281–301.

Ostrom, E. 1990. *Governing the Commons.* Cambridge, U.K.: Cambridge University Press.

Samuelson, P. 1954. "The Pure Theory of Public Expenditures." *Review of Economics and Statistics* 36: 387–89.

Sandler, T. 1997. *Global Challenges: An Approach to Environmental, Political, and Economic Problems.* Cambridge, U.K.: Cambridge University Press.

Schelling, T. C. 1960. *The Strategy of Conflict.* Cambridge, Massachusetts: Harvard University Press.

Sobel, D. 1995. *Longitude.* New York: Walker.

Chapter 4

FINANCING INTERNATIONAL PUBLIC GOODS

Todd Sandler

In recent years the World Bank, the United Nations (UN), and other international organizations have recognized the growing importance of international public goods (IPGs) to their missions.[1] IPGs possess benefits that spill over national borders so that their benefits extend beyond the country of origin. Provision of these goods represents a novel rationale for foreign assistance that transcends country-based motives, because the donor may also gain from the good's benefits (Ferroni 2000; Jayaraman and Kanbur 1999; Kanbur, Sandler, and Morrison 1999; Sandler 1997). Technology continues to provide new forms of public goods whose benefits cross political and generational boundaries.[2] When an IPG is purely public, both payers and nonpayers receive its benefits, and one person's consumption does not necessarily reduce the benefits available to others from the same unit of the good. In the extreme case of global public goods (GPGs), the good's benefits disperse worldwide, for instance, efforts to curb global warming, to reduce ozone depleting chlorofluorocarbon (CFC) emissions, to map the human genome, or to preserve the earth's biodiversity. IPGs are associated with a wide range of activities involving the environment, security, financial stability, scientific discovery, health care, infrastructure, poverty reduction, culture preservation, and research and development.

Given this heightened interest in the study of IPGs and their allocative and distributional implications, a key concern is how to finance the provision of these IPGs. Should the world community rely on voluntary efforts to finance IPGs at the national level? Should it instead engineer a collective response?

Or should it employ a combination of voluntary national provision and collective financing? The answers to these questions hinge on the nature of the public good.

Understanding that the three dimensions of "publicness"—nonexcludability of nonpayers, nonrivalry of benefits, and the manner in which contributions determine aggregate provision (the aggregation technology)—influence the possibilities for financing IPGs is essential. The aggregation technology dimension of publicness goes beyond the two classical properties of nonrivalry and nonexcludability and is instrumental in understanding policy recommendations (for example, the use of taxes for public provision in the presence of private provision) and institutional design (Bucholz and Konrad 1995; Cornes 1993; Sandler 1997, 1998; Sandler and Sargent 1995; Vicary 1990). For some public goods these properties are such that a public sector "push" is needed, or else the good will not be financed. This push can come in the form of a supranational structure, such as the World Bank, the UN, or the European Union (EU), which collects the required fees from its members to underwrite these IPGs. In some instances the leader nation(s) might provide the required push and funding, which may only be germane initially, because voluntary financing may become adequate as nations gain experience with an IPG or develop a capacity or a need to use the good's benefits. Other properties of IPGs may promote market incentives or voluntary contributions, so that only a little public sector coaxing is necessary. For still other IPGs, incentives are consistent with the operation of markets or clubs, so that no official intervention is required as the IPGs are financed through unofficial means with few transaction costs.

To understand the role of international institutions in promoting IPGs, one must ascertain the nature of the good and whether it requires a push, coaxing, or no assistance from a supranational structure or influential nation(s) and agents, for instance, charitable foundations. Resources are scarce in the international community, and a reliance on markets and clubs, when feasible, will reduce burdens by channeling resources to those IPGs whose financing is the most problematic. At the national level, governments support public goods provision through taxes levied on their citizens, but a reliance on taxes imposed by a supranational government on subordinate nations is typically not an option. (An exception is the EU, which has the power to collect tax revenues from its member governments.)

Nevertheless, IPGs are provided and underwritten either through charges levied by supranational organizations or clubs or through voluntary contributions. In many cases the level of provision of IPGs will be inadequate given their far-ranging spillover of benefits. This chapter looks at alternative means and institutional arrangements for financing IPGs. If the world community is to support IPGs adequately, then an understanding of these arrangements is essential. Spawned by technology, novel IPGs appear often and present allocative challenges that must be addressed.

This chapter has five objectives. The first is to review some basic principles of public finance involving national and local public goods that can guide supranational financing of IPGs.[3] The second is to relate these principles to a taxonomy of IPGs that indicates the financing possibilities for each of five basic kinds of IPGs distinguished by the nature of their benefits. The third is to associate financing possibilities to the aggregation technology whereby individual contributions determine the overall level of IPGs. The fourth is to identify further considerations that can guide a society's quest for effective financial schemes. The fifth is to show how a variety of supranational and other institutions have put these financing principles into practice in their provision of IPGs.

BASIC TAXATION PRINCIPLES FOR FINANCING PUBLIC GOODS

Some principles of taxation apply to the national provision of public goods when voluntary or private provision is inadequate. The public sector is involved in two essential activities: providing public goods and redistributing income to satisfy some ethical norm of fairness (Bruce 1998). Although distinguishing between these activities is convenient, they are inter-related; thus the manner in which a public good is provided has clear distributional consequences, while a change in income distribution may itself be a public good. Two overall principles of taxation guide the financing of public goods at the national level and can be applied to IPGs at the supranational level.

The benefit principle requires that the recipients of a good's benefits pay their marginal willingness to pay (MWTP) or the value of their marginal benefit from consuming the good. If all consumers pays their MWTP, and if the sum of the MWTP collected is equal to the public good's marginal cost of provision, an optimal level of a pure public good is then provided, because social benefits match social costs at the margin. For pure public goods where benefits are nonrival and nonexcludable, agents do not willingly reveal their MWTP, thus the benefit principle may prove impractical to implement. The provider's failure to exclude nonpayers and to monitor use is what makes tying charges for pure public goods to consumers' MWTP exceedingly difficult. If asked to reveal their MWTP, consumers will understate their derived pleasure in an attempt to limit their payment for the good. A completely different situation characterizes private goods that people can only acquire by paying the market price. Agents purchase a private good until their MWTP, captured by the height of the points on their demand curve, equals the good's price. This price equals marginal cost under competitive provision, so that individuals automatically satisfy the benefit principle through their voluntary purchases of private goods.

Most public goods are not purely public, and permit either some exclusion or some rivalry of benefits. If the public good's benefits can be withheld from nonpayers, then the private sector may be able to provide the good without public sector intervention. For example, golf courses are both privately and publicly provided, as are parks and schools. Private provision is possible for a golf course, because each round of golf can be monitored and a fee charged. Public provision and financing is best reserved for those situations where exclusion is inadequate and private provision is not feasible. For some activities both private and public benefits are simultaneously derived. Schooling benefits not only the individual with private marketable skills, but it also improves social well-being with enhanced demands for culture and/or law and order. If these private benefits are a sufficiently large share of total benefits, then private provision is possible. Private provision works best when the nature of the public good permits fees, collected from users, to be based on a benefit principle where aggregate MTWP is equated to the good's marginal cost of provision.

A second way to finance a public good when private alternatives are unavailable is to base agents' financial burden in relation to the good on their ability to pay. From an administrative viewpoint an ability to pay scheme does not require the government to ascertain the agents' MWTP schedules, and is therefore not expected to achieve optimal provision of the public good. Efficiency is sacrificed for practical implementation. The actual relationship between ability to pay and assigned burdens reflects alternative notions of fairness. One such concept is horizontal equity, which requires people with the same income or wealth to carry identical burdens for the public good. Quite simply, equals should be treated equally. In the U.S. tax system, the so-called marriage penalty is a clear violation of horizontal equity. An alternative fairness criterion is vertical equity, in which agents with higher incomes are made to finance a greater amount of the public good through taxes or assigned assessments. This criterion introduces distributional equity founded on an analogy with the utilitarian concept of diminishing marginal utility of income, where a dollar taken from a richer agent has less of an impact on an agent's well-being than a dollar taken from someone poorer.

Of these two equity criteria, vertical equity is more prevalent as a guiding influence for ability to pay schemes. Progressive income taxation, where richer people pay a larger percentage of their income in taxes than poorer individuals, is an instance of vertical equity. Membership dues to learned societies that are graduated based on income, for example, dues to belong to the American Economic Association and the American Political Science Association, preserve vertical equity where the shared public goods are the societies' journals and infrastructure. Property taxes are another means of applying vertical equity by collecting more in taxes from those with greater wealth. Some supranational structures that rely on an ability to pay financing arrangement also apply the vertical equity principle. When a push is needed, governments usually resort to an ability to pay arrangement that incorporates some criteria of fairness.

A TAXONOMY AND FINANCING POSSIBILITIES

The literature presents various taxonomies for public goods depending on the purposes and properties of the goods being studied (see, for example, Kanbur, Sandler, and Morrison 1999; Sandler 1999). Table 4.1 presents five alternative categories of IPGs, distinguished according to how such goods fulfill the two properties of pure publicness.

Pure Public Goods

If the good's benefits are both nonrival and nonexcludable, then the good is a pure public good. A good's benefits are nonrival among users when one agent's consumption or use of the good does not detract, in the slightest, from the

Table 4.1. Alternative Types of and Financing Possibilities for IPGs

Good type	Examples	Financing possibilities	Remarks
Pure public	• Curbing global warming • Basic research • Limiting the spread of disease • Augmenting the ozone shield	Usually must rely on some kind of public sector push based on an ability to pay charge. Financing coordinated by a supra-national organization using some international taxation or fee arrangement. A leader nation or nations might exist if sufficient net benefits can be derived.	Neutrality worries arise, because voluntary contributions will be crowded out by collective contributions. Partial coopera-tion faces free-riding offsets in the absence of sufficient participation. An enforcement mechanism is necessary.
Impurely public with some rivalry, but no exclusion	• Ocean fisheries • Controlling pests • Curbing organized crime • Alleviating acid rain	Must again rely on supranational organizations and some international collection arrangement. Rivalry may motivate more independent behavior in contrast to purely public goods.	More private incentives to contribute. Rivalry lessens neutrality concerns, but a push from the public sector is still required.
Impurely public with some exclusion	• Missile defense system • Disaster relief aid • Extension services • Information dissemination	Exclusion promotes voluntary financing and club-like structures. For these goods the public sector may be needed for coaxing and facilitating eventual private sector provision. There may exist an entre-preneurial or leader nation to market the good.	Because exclusion is not complete, some suboptimality remains. The question is whether this residual suboptimality warrants any intervention or official inducements.

Club good	• Transnational parks • INTELSAT • Remote sensing services • Canals, other waterways	Charge each use according to the crowding that results. Nonpayers are excluded. Toll per use is equal to marginal crowding costs so as to internalize the congestion externality. Taste differences can be reflected by tolls paid on total visits. Nations with a greater demand visit more often and pay more than those with a smaller demand.	Can result in an efficient outcome. Clubs limit transaction costs. Full financing depends on scale economies, the form of the congestion functions, and other considerations (for example, competitiveness of factor or output markets). No public coaxing is needed.
Joint products	• Foreign aid • Tropical forests • Peacekeeping • Defense spending among allies	As nation-specific private benefits and club good benefits become more prevalent among the joint products, markets and club arrangements can be used to finance the good with greater efficiency. As the share of excludable benefits increases, payments can be increasingly based on benefits received.	Ratio of excludable to total benefits is the essential consideration. As this ratio approaches one, markets and clubs work more fully. Institutional arrangements can foster these excludable benefits.

Source: Author.

consumption opportunities still available to other agents from the same unit of the good. For example, reducing CFCs or greenhouse gas emissions helps stem the depletion of the ozone layer and the heating of the atmosphere, respectively, which affect all nations. If a provider of a public good cannot keep an agent, such as an individual, a firm, or a nation, from receiving the good's benefits, then its benefits are nonexcludable. The provider cannot, therefore, keep a nonpayer from taking advantage of the good's benefits, and this inability limits users' incentives to finance the good's provision. Again consider the reduction of CFCs and greenhouse gases. Nations engaged in these reductions cannot deny other nations from receiving the benefits that result. Thus curbing global warming and improving the protective stratospheric ozone shield are purely public, because both activities' benefits are nonrival and nonexcludable.

Two additional examples of pure public goods at the transnational level are limiting the spread of contagious diseases such as AIDS and ebola and uncovering basic research findings. Efforts to forestall the spread of a contagious disease benefit all those at risk regardless of whether or not they supported the containment. In addition, the reduced risk one person gains from prophylactic measures does not limit the protection afforded to others. Once made public, basic research findings will diffuse rapidly among those with the capacity to understand them. Even before being released, information about basic research findings tends to leak out to the scientific community. The findings are nonrival and can be exploited to advantage by countless teams of researchers without diminishing their benefits. For example, the discovery of calculus provided a mathematical tool that one researcher can use without limiting its application by others.

The last two columns of table 4.1 show financing possibilities and remarks for each of the five categories of IPGs. Financing is most problematic for pure public goods. A best-case scenario would be a leader nation that derives sufficient benefits to justify its provision of the good, even if it is the only one bearing the costs, for example, U.S. efforts to underwrite the Centers for Disease Control. In the absence of a leader nation, the global community will have to resort to a supranational structure, such as the UN, that subsequently charges its members based on some ability to pay measure. Currently, no transnational public finance system exists whereby taxes collected on, say, internationally traded items (the so-called Tobin tax) could be earmarked to finance IPGs, thus supranational structures must provide the required push to fund these goods.

With pure public goods a concern with neutrality always arises, where collective provision or financing crowds out voluntary national provision on a dollar-for-dollar basis (see Cornes and Sandler 1996, chapter 6; Warr 1983). Thus efforts to augment national provision with collective provision will fail to increase the overall supply of public goods if the voluntary contributors are made to fund the collective efforts.[4] This neutrality or crowding-out problem arises because one contributor's provision of a pure public good is a perfect substitute for that from other contributors. Increased provision, no matter how it is financed, replaces the need to contribute on one's own. Neutrality has disturbing implications for financing a pure public good either through income redistribution from small providers to large providers or tax-financed official support of IPGs with taxes levied on contributors. Neutrality indicates that engineered redistributions of income among contributors have no net impact on the supply of IPGs; those receiving income merely increase their IPG contributions by the amount that those losing income decrease their contributions. For purely public goods, contributors view public good benefit spillovers from others as equivalent to extra income. To maintain their well-being, nations merely let the increased public goods supply by others make up for their income losses stemming from taxes or redistribution. Only a tax imposed on a noncontributor can result in more of the public good, but at the expense of social welfare if the noncontributor has little taste for the IPG. An efficiency loss arises, because the tax burden on the noncontributor outweighs any gain derived from the augmented IPG supply if the noncontributor has little desire for the good.

Another consideration has to do with partial cooperation, whereby some nations choose not to be part of a collective agreement or supranational organization established to provide more of a pure IPG. These noncooperators can partly or wholly offset the increased contributions by deliberately contributing less in response to cooperation-induced increases in provision (Buchholz, Haslbeck, and Sandler 1998). Three factors bolster the success of partial cooperative financing of a purely public good: (a) a large number of cooperating countries, (b) noncooperators with a relatively low (high) valuation of the private (public) good, and (c) a large proportion of noncooperators who are minor contributors. Such factors provide little ability for the noncooperators to undo the efforts of like-minded cooperators by cutting back on their support for the IPG. Factor (a) implies that there are fewer noncooperators to counter efforts at cooperation, while factor (b) indicates that noncooperators have little incentive to reduce their IPG provision in response to partial cooperation. Finally, factor (c) means that only small cutbacks are possible, as noncooperators are minor contributors prior to a cooperative arrangement, which does not include them. Such a partial agreement can finance the IPG through cost shares assigned to each country based on ability to pay, given the lack of incentives to truthfully reveal MWTP. Even with cost-sharing agreements to supply more of an IPG, an enforcement mechanism may be required, which presents yet an additional collective action concern as to how the cooperators will finance such a mechanism (Heckathorn 1989).

Impure Public Goods

When IPGs possess benefits that are either partially nonrival or partially excludable, that is, excludable at a cost, they are impurely public. The second category of public goods in table 4.1 consists of impure IPGs that display some rivalry, but whose benefits are still nonexcludable. Such goods include ocean fisheries where property rights may be difficult to protect or that are owned in common, so that benefits still have a strong element of nonexcludability. Rivalry applies because increased fishing efforts limit the catch of others through crowding. That is, each fishing vessel must exert a greater effort to haul in the same catch as the efforts of others increase. Controlling pests, curbing organized crime, and alleviating acid rain display rivalry, as efforts by one individual influence the benefits available for others. For pests, control applied in one place cannot also be applied elsewhere, and results in the pest population decreasing where the action is taken and increasing where it is not. Efforts directed at thwarting organized crime in one place may merely displace the criminal activity to a less protected venue, so that benefits are rival through the consumption process. Improvements to the environment or to security within a society stemming from these activities are, however, nonexcludable. Without excludability this class of goods may at times be difficult to support through voluntary actions, so that either some push is needed from a supranational organization or a leader nation is required. Rivalry, however, limits neutrality, because contributions are less substitutable, and for some cases sufficient private inducements to promote contributions may even result. If, for example, a nation's efforts to control sulfur emissions primarily curtail acid rain over its own territory, because of a spatial rivalry (that is, every ton of emissions dropped on it cannot fall elsewhere) some voluntary action can be anticipated (Murdoch, Sandler, and Sargent 1997).

The remaining three categories of IPGs in table 4.1 all have a better prognosis for financing without the need for some elaborate supranational structure, either because of excludable benefits or private nation-specific gains. For these three cases, either coaxing or no help is needed from a transnational public sector. Impure IPGs with some excludable benefits—for instance, a missile defense system, disaster relief aid, extension services, and information dissemination—can be withheld from nonpayers. Thus whether or not a country is protected by a missile defense system or whether it receives extension services hinges on its own provision or its willingness to pay a provider for these excludable benefits. Exclusion promotes voluntary financing and club-like structures where use can be monitored and charged a fee. Because exclusion is not complete, some suboptimality remains. Consider information dissemination where controlling whether or not one buyer can freely pass on the acquired information to a nonpayer may be difficult. Even for missile defense, protection may not be denied to a nonpayer when collateral damage to the provider would result from an attack on the nonpayer. An ideal club arrangement charges a toll to internalize the crowding externality associated with rivalry, but for this third kind of IPG, rivalry may not be involved, and this presents a problem, for example, possession of information by one nation need not result in rivalry for another if the information can be easily provided whenever needed (on clubs and their toll arrangements see Buchanan 1965; Cornes and Sandler 1996, chapters 11–13; Sandler and Tschirhart 1997).

Club Goods

Club goods represent the fourth kind of IPG and hold out the greatest promise for self-financing without an elaborate structure or guidance from a supranational body. If the exclusion cost is sufficiently small to allow utilization rates to be monitored and users to be charged a toll or user fee, then the users can form a club and provide themselves with the shared good. Nonmembers are excluded from the benefits of the club good, while members pay a toll for each use or visit equal to the marginal crowding cost that results. In this way the toll internalizes the crowding externality, and resources are directed toward their most valued use.

A member visits the club and pays the user fee only when the member's resulting gain is at least as great as the toll that must be paid per visit. Even taste differences among members are taken into account: members with a stronger preference for the club good will visit more often and will thus pay more in total tolls, so that preferences are automatically revealed. Club members are charged their MWTP, therefore club pricing abides by a benefit principle. For clubs to function properly there must be an exclusion device that is inexpensive to operate along with crowding or rivalry in consumption that requires internalizing. If the scale of the club is insufficient to accommodate all nations, then multiple clubs can be replicated so that every nation finds itself in a club of optimum size (Sandler and Tschirhart 1997).[5]

Clubs provide an institutional alternative to creating elaborate supranational structures or taxing authorities. Given that nations cherish their sovereignty, they are loathe to agree to supranational taxation as a means of financing IPGs. Clubs are relatively simple structures that require little more than an exclusion mechanism or a toll booth so that the transaction cost is economized. Once income or sales taxes are used to finance IPGs, the link between who receives the goods' benefits and who finances them is severed, so that allocative inefficiency results. Clubs maintain this connection between benefits and financing through their toll charges, because only those members whose MWTP justifies paying the toll will use the facilities, and then only to the point at which a member's MWTP just equals the toll.

Full financing of optimal provision of the club good depends on congestion, production, and competitive considerations. The form of the crowding function is an important determinant in ascertaining whether or not the toll can fully finance the club good (Cornes and Sandler 1996, pp. 391–93; DeSerpa 1978; Oakland 1972). If the crowding function is homogeneous of degree zero in provision and utilization, so that a doubling of use and facility size leaves crowding unchanged, then an optimal toll will self-finance the club whenever competitive conditions prevail and production of the club good is not under increasing returns to scale. This follows because a toll set equal to the marginal crowding cost associated with a visit takes in enough on each unit of the shared good to finance the marginal cost of provision (Siqueira and Sandler 2001; Small 1999).[6] If constant cost prevails, then the cost per unit equals marginal cost, and the proceeds collected on each unit also cover average cost. The tolls derived from all units provided will then just cover total provision cost. When increasing cost or decreasing returns to scale apply, marginal cost exceeds average cost, and a toll that earns enough to cover the former will more than finance the shared good. If, however, increasing returns to scale characterize the production of the public good, then a per unit toll that finances marginal cost is insufficient to cover average cost. A two-part toll is then required, with the shortfall in financing being made up by a fixed membership charge.

When competitive factor markets do not hold, monopsony may exist in the buying of inputs, which implies a rising factor supply curve (Small 1999). For an IPG such as peacekeeping or peace enforcement, some factors, such as titanium used to strengthen weapons systems, may have monopsonistic elements. Such a noncompetitive consideration results in a toll that overfinances provision as the rising factor supply curve diminishes economies of scale of cost, thereby leading the ratio of average to marginal cost to be less than one. If the toll per unit covers marginal cost, it will then cover average cost.

Examples of club IPGs include transnational parks such as the Great Barrier Reef off the coast of Australia and tracts of pristine rain forest worldwide. Even national parks qualify as transnational because of their international visitors. These parks use toll schemes to finance land acquisition, park infrastructure, and park maintenance. INTELSAT, a private consortium of nations and firms, operates as a club to share a communications satellite network in geostationary orbit that carries most international phone calls and television transmissions. Data from remote sensing satellites, for example, LANDSAT surveying, are sold to users in a club-like arrangement based on individual demands for surveys. Canals and waterways like the Suez Canal and the St. Lawrence Seaway permit exclusion and monitoring, and thus also represent club IPGs.

Joint Products

The final category of IPGs consists of joint products that simultaneously yield two or more outputs that may vary in their degree of publicness. Joint products may be purely public, impurely public, or private. As nation-specific private and club good benefits become a greater share of the joint products, market and club arrangements can be applied to finance the activity, thereby eliminating the need for any push or coaxing from some governmental body. Suppose that only nation-specific benefits characterize the joint products. Recipient nations have a clear incentive to reveal their MWTP through payments for the IPG.

Quite simply, nation-specific benefits, which are private among nations though possibly public within recipient nations, serve as a privatizing influence, not unlike the establishment of property rights. Next suppose that both a nation-specific private benefit and a global pure public benefit are produced jointly by the public activity. If these jointly produced outputs are complementary so that nations desire to consume them together, then markets can sell the activity as a package based on a benefit principle applied to the private good component and use the proceeds to finance the entire activity. If club outputs are prevalent, then these can be charged tolls (Sandler 1977). The essential determinant for financing joint products is the ratio of excludable benefits (nation-specific and club benefits) to total benefits. As this ratio approaches one so that all benefits are excludable, markets and clubs can be employed to finance the activity without elaborate and costly supranational structures. The closer the ratio is to one, the more relevant is a benefit principle of financing.

In many ways joint products may include all the other categories as special cases. If, for example, an activity yields only a single excludable and rival output, then it is a private good. If, however, it yields only a purely public output, then it is a pure public good. When an activity provides both private and public goods, it is neither purely private or public, so that a new category of goods is needed. This new class is called joint products. In practice, many activities give rise to multiple outputs that vary in their degree of publicness.

Table 4.1 lists instances of joint products. For example, poverty reduction in the form of foreign assistance can provide donor-specific benefits if the aid is tied or conditional. In addition, any poverty that this aid relieves yields a GPG for all richer countries concerned with the well-being of those less fortunate. Even without conditional aid, a donor can derive benefits from an IPG's output that protects its citizens, as in the case of containing an epidemic abroad so as to eliminate it before it arrives on the donor's own soil. Joint products also characterize the rain forests, whose preservation generates purely public benefits worldwide because of carbon sequestration and biodiversity. Host country and regional benefits from these rain forests include erosion control, localized climate effects, watersheds, and ecotourist sites. Such localized benefits provide these tropical countries with a stake in their forest preservation and, in so doing, should motivate some action. Peacekeeping provides nation-specific benefits for nations nearest to an unstable situation, and also yields more global pure public benefits to the world community in terms of enhanced political security, reduced trade disruptions, and curtailment of human suffering.

Migrations and other collateral effects may affect nations near areas of conflict. Defense shared among allies provides pure public benefits by deterring an attack and nation-specific benefits from arms devoted to curbing domestic terrorism or maintaining colonial control.

AGGREGATION TECHNOLOGIES OF PUBLIC SUPPLY

To address the possibilities for public goods financing, one must consider more than just the nonrivalry and nonexcludability of benefits. A third essential characteristic of publicness involves how individual contributions to the public good determine the total quantity of the good available for consumption, a relationship we will refer to as aggregation technology.[7] This aggregation concept influences the incentives that the potential contributors possess and, in so doing, affects financing and other policy concerns related to the provision of public goods. A rich variety of alternative aggregation technologies exists; however, this chapter discusses only four (table 4.2).

Summation

The most common technology is that of summation, where each unit contributed to the public good adds identically and cumulatively to the level of the good available to all for consumption. Because each unit has the same marginal impact on total provision, one agent's contribution is a perfect substitute for that of another agent. Table 4.2 provides three examples of a summation technology. In the case of ambient air pollution, such as methane resulting from agriculture and mining, total emissions in the atmosphere equal the sum of the pollutants emitted by various sources. Air quality is cumulatively affected by individual emissions. Similarly, efforts to improve air quality by reducing methane emissions correspond to the sum of individual cutbacks. The accumulation of greenhouse gases also abides by an additive technology of aggregation. If 1,000 nations each emit 500 metric tons of greenhouse gases into the atmosphere, the 500,000-metric ton accumulation heats the atmosphere. Each metric ton adds identically to global warming. When species are cataloged, each species identified adds a new single entry to the total.

Table 4.2. Alternative Aggregation Technologies of Public Supply

Supply technology	Examples	Strategic considerations	Institutional implications
Summation: public good level equals the sum of individual contributions	• Curbing air pollution • Reducing global warming • Cataloging species	Characterized often by prisoners' dilemma or chicken game form. In the former, there are strong incentives to free-ride and not contribute; in the latter, the richest have an incentive to inhibit dire consequences.	In an assistance context, a multilateral organization or rich nation is needed to assume leadership and to provide the public good. Cannot typically rely on voluntary action at the national level.
Weakest link: only the smallest effort determines the public good level	• Containing river blindness • Maintaining the integrity of networks • Limiting the spread of insurrections	Assurance games where matching behavior characterizes the equilibriums. Actions and/or contracts are self-enforcing. Well-endowed players have an incentive to assist those less well-off.	Multilateral agencies can channel funds and direct actions to raise public good levels to acceptable standards. Capacity building required in poor countries. Rich countries may contribute the public good directly to increase levels in poorer countries. Partnerships apply.
Best shot: only the largest effort determines the public good level	• Finding a cure for AIDS • Neutralizing a pest • Engineering the next green revolution	Coordination games where only a single provider is required. Problem of identifying this agent if there are two or more candidates; this is where coordination is needed. For development concerns, problems arise when the best-endowed nation derives little benefit from the action.	Put supply efforts where the prospects and resources are the greatest for success. Multilateral organizations or a leader nation can serve to coalesce and focus resources and efforts. Partnerships among various participants can circumvent collective action problems.
Weighted sum: each country's contribution can have a different additive impact	• Cleanup of sulfur emissions • Monitoring Earth from different vantages • Controlling a pest	Weighted sum implies that some participants receive greater private benefits, and thus have greater inducements to contribute. Captures pure public and private good representations as special cases. A host of alternative game forms.	Multilateral organizations need to support efforts among only those nations with less country-specific benefits. Collect and provide information on the weight matrix to encourage independent financing.

Source: Author.

When a classic public goods problem is considered, often there is an implicit assumption that a summation technology applies. This technology was so ingrained in public goods thinking that other aggregation possibilities and their strategic implications were not even considered until Hirshleifer's (1983) contribution. Two game forms typically underlie the summation representation of a public good. The first is the prisoners' dilemma, where each potential contributor has a dominant strategy (no matter what the other contributors do) to free-ride on the contributions of others (Sandler 1992). This follows because contributors consider just the difference between the benefits and costs that they derive from a unit contributed and ignore benefits conferred on others. Suppose that each unit of the public good provides each of five potential contributors with US\$6 in benefits at a cost of US\$8 to just the provider of the unit. Even though a unit yields US\$30 (US\$6 × number of people receiving benefits) in total benefits, a potential contributor will view the transaction as yielding –US\$2 (own benefit of US\$6 – own cost of US\$8) and opt not to contribute. If all potential participants view payoffs like this, then everyone will free-ride and nothing will be contributed. To escape this dilemma for IPGs, one or more nations must gain sufficient benefits, beyond those of the average nation, to provide the public good. This may be the case when some contributors are richer and place greater value on the public good (Olson 1965; Sandler 1992). A second escape can come from an organized effort by a multilateral organization to collect the necessary funds to provide the public good.

The second game form that can apply is a chicken game for a summation technology where per unit cost is again less than per unit benefit when viewed from an individual contributor's perspective. The difference in the chicken representation is that doing nothing at all, or doing too little, results in negative payoffs, that is, some of the public good must be provided or everyone suffers. Not contributing is no longer a dominant strategy. If, for instance, nothing at all is done about a pollution problem, the consequences may be dire. The same may be the case for an emerging plague. One or more nations will have incentives to accomplish some minimal sufficient effort to forestall the disaster. The most likely contributors are the best endowed nations or a multilateral agency that can direct efforts.

When combined with nonrival and nonexcludable benefits, a summation technology results in financing worries for IPGs and the need for transnational public sector coordination.

Weakest Link

For a weakest link technology, the smallest contribution level fixes the quantity of the public good for the entire group. When controlling a contagious disease such as river blindness (onchocerciasis), a nation expending the least efforts at containment determines the risk to neighboring nations of the disease spreading (by a parasitic worm carried by a fly). Hirshleifer's (1983) classic paper illustrated the concept of weakest link using the example of dikes along the coastline of a circular island, where flood protection hinged on the height of the lowest levee. Another example is the integrity of a network, where the least reliable part determines the reliability of the entire network. When a nation is confronted with an insurrection, the province with the least effective defense sets the safety standard of the entire nation by allowing the rebels to gain a base from which to launch their attacks. Yet another example concerns tracking the progress of a disease or a pest where the monitoring station least up to the task determines the authority's ability to know the progress of the disease or pest. Currently, the United States is seriously contemplating improving the Russian early warning system, which is in disrepair, so that Russia never wrongly thinks that it is under attack.

Because of an inherent complementary, incentives are more favorable for the international community to supply, and even finance, other countries' weakest link public goods. For such IPGs, incentives exist for each nation to match the smallest contribution, because larger contributions use up scarce resources without augmenting the level of the IPG. An assurance game applies where it is in each nation's interests to match other nations' contributions to a weakest link IPG, because failing to do so makes individual nations worse off (Sandler 1992; Sandler and Sargent 1995, p. 153).[8] Unlike the prisoners' dilemma, contracts are self-enforcing, because once one nation delivers its IPG provision, others can only prosper by doing the same. Rich nations are also induced to form partnerships with poorer countries to raise their level of a weakest link IPG to more acceptable standards (Ferroni 2000; Vicary and Sandler forthcoming). Ferroni correctly indicates that these partnerships are complex and difficult to achieve, but the incentives are nevertheless right for doing so. Moreover, it is an easy political sell to the rich country's constituency that foreign assistance to improve, say, the fight against an infectious disease, provides safety at home. Partnerships to foster the financing of these weakest link IPGs can be either bilateral or multilateral. Supranational organizations such as the World Health Organization (WHO) can coordinate such partnerships.

The recognition of weakest link IPGs provides a whole new rationale for foreign assistance. When a wealthy country has both funds and a comparative advantage in providing the IPG, the best approach is for it to provide such increases of a weakest link IPG directly until the recipient builds up its own capacity (Buchholz and Konrad 1995; Jayaraman and Kanbur 1999; Vicary and Sandler forthcoming). Over time, the donor country should foster the recipient country's capacity to provide its own weakest link IPG. It is in the interests of donor countries to build up recipient countries' provision and financing capacity with respect to weakest link IPGs, especially when a large number of countries have insufficient capacity.

Best Shot

Best shot represents a third basic aggregation technology for which the largest contribution of an individual sets the aggregate level of the IPG available for consumption. When finding a cure for AIDS, malaria, or other diseases, the research team expending the largest effort is most apt to meet with the success that benefits everyone at risk. Once a cure is uncovered, further efforts achieve little or nothing. Similarly, engineering successful neutralization of a pest through a clever strategy, for example, mating flies with sterile females released into the environment, eliminates the threat for everyone. Further research and other strategies are then unnecessary. A third example is the engineering of the next green revolution, which is likely to be discovered by the team with the greatest research budget and the best scientists. In general, scientific and health breakthroughs abide by a best shot aggregation technology.

The underlying game is that of coordination, where just a single provider is needed and potential suppliers must decide among themselves which should expend the effort (Sandler 1998; Sandler and Sargent 1995). Coordination problems are particularly tricky in the presence of more than one best shot candidate, because resources may be wasted if multiple efforts merely duplicate a discovery or fall short of discoveries required to unlock the mystery. A number of institutional implications are associated with best shot (table 4.2). Supply efforts should be concentrated where prospects and existing resources are the greatest for success. If potential contributors have an equal likelihood of success, then multiple providers may make sense unless combining contributors' efforts augments the likelihood of success, a likely scenario with best shot. With best shot there is a rationale for assisting the efforts of a rich nation or forming a partnership among diverse participants. For a best shot IPG in the health sector, partners might include drug companies, a host country, rich donor countries, and multilateral agencies. The prognosis is less optimistic when rich potential donors have less direct interest in a best shot IPG. In the case of malaria, which is ravaging developing tropical countries, rich countries have displayed ennui, because malaria poses little threat to their populations. Seeing little prospect for profit, until recently drug companies have not put much effort into finding a cure. Such best shot IPGs that do not involve rich countries need financing support from multilateral organizations such as the World Bank. Such goods do not possess the right incentives, and thus need a public sector push. Partnerships can also be spearheaded by such organizations, as in the case of the Medicines for Malaria Venture.

Weighted Sum

A fourth aggregate technology consists of weighted sum for which the weights in the sum are no longer one in value, as in the case of a summation technology. Weighted sum generalizes summation technology. Individual contributions possess weights, which reflect the marginal impact that a unit of a contributor's provision has for total provision of the IPG. For acid rain, the cleanup of sulfur emissions from power plants and vehicles adheres to weighted sum, as the location of the source of the pollutants affects the pattern of dispersion of downwind depositions because of wind direction (Murdoch, Sandler, and Sargent 1997). Countries farther from the source of a cleanup gain smaller reductions in their acid rain deposits, compared with a less distant downwind neighbor. Monitoring the planet at various vantage points yields aggregate intelligence, whose total is differentially impacted by the stations' location. Efforts to control a pest may also adhere to weighted sum if the distribution of the pest is unequal, so that eradication efforts in its stronghold yield greater results than where the pest is less prevalent. With weighted sum, some nations receive disproportionately greater benefits, and thus possess a large incentive to support the IPG. Efforts should be channeled to where provision has the greatest marginal impact.

A wide variety of game forms and strategic implications are associated with a weighted sum technology, partly because weighted sum can include summation (all weights are one) and private goods (the weight on the providing nation's provision is one and it is zero on all other potential recipients). In the former case, the prisoners' dilemma or chicken games are relevant underlying games, while in the latter, incentives exist for the country that benefits to supply its own private good. Depending on the weights, assurance or coordination interactions may apply where either matching behavior results or some dominant nation or group of nations provides the IPG. The greater the country-specific benefits derived from a weighted sum IPG, that is, the larger the weight on its provision, the greater its inducement to contribute. When weights are no longer one, contributions are no longer substitutable, and there is no concern that public effort, coordinated by multilaterals, crowds out contributions from individual nations. Thus some patterns of weights may promote IPG funding, thereby either limiting the required public sector push or making such a push more effective when needed.

Multilaterals can further these self-financing incentives by providing the information required to compute the weights. This is precisely what the Cooperative Programme for Monitoring and Evaluation has done in Europe. Funded by the UN, the program has determined the weight matrix associated with sulfur emissions, nitrogen oxides, and other pollutants.

Thus this third property of publicness has much to say about whether or not incentives support voluntary provision and financing of an IPG. When financing is unlikely, aggregation technologies help define the role that a supranational structure or a nation's leadership can play in collecting the necessary financing.

TWO ADDITIONAL FINANCING CONSIDERATIONS

Additional financing considerations involve economies of scope and the principle of subsidiarity.

Economies of Scope

In practice, many supranational structures address more than a single IPG allocation problem. For example, the World Bank not only provides foreign assistance to alleviate poverty and promote development, but it also produces basic research. The UN promotes peacekeeping, alleviates hunger, tracks population growth, furthers world health, and facilitates environmental protection. Even a military alliance like the North Atlantic Treaty Organization (NATO) pursues a host of public goods in addition to deterrence, including traffic control, navigation, drug interdiction, and scientific research (Sandler and Hartley 2001). Yet other supranational structures, such as the EU, the International Monetary Fund, and the Organisation for Economic Co-operation and Development, also supply multiple public goods.

What factors are at work in such organizations that encourage them to provide more than one IPG? The answer involves economies of scope, which occur when the cost of providing two or more IPGs jointly in the same institution is cheaper than supplying them in separate institutions. Such scope economies stem from common cost attributable to IPGs. If two IPGs can use the same administrative staff, communication network, meeting facilities, research staff, and scientific personnel, then cost in common arises from shared inputs. Underutilized infrastructure may be the source of some economies of scope. As an infrastructure reaches full capacity, a supranational structure must decide if enlarging its capacity to accommodate additional IPGs is cheaper, or whether assigning new IPG decisions to either specialized institutions under its oversight or to independent institutions is more reasonable. Both practices are used. For example, the International Maritime Organization (IMO) and the International Telecommunication Union (ITU) are specialized UN agencies. In contrast, the World Court, which facilitates dispute settlements over property rights, and the World Trade Organization, which facilitates dispute settlements over trade, both evolved as new institutions.

Subsidiarity

In a now classic paper, Olson (1969) presented the concept of fiscal equivalence, where those affected by the spillovers of a public good should be the ones who decide its allocation and financing. Quite simply, the decisionmaking jurisdiction should coincide with the region of spillovers so that only those who are affected get to express their preferences. Financing equivalence would dictate that the financial burden for the IPG should only affect those receiving its benefits. When the political jurisdiction exceeds the range of spillovers, taxes are then imposed on people (nations) that do not benefit, thereby motivating oversupply by those making the decision. If, in contrast, the political jurisdiction is a proper subset of the IPG's range of spillovers, then undersupply is anticipated, because benefits conferred on those outside the political jurisdiction are ignored. When, for example, an IPG benefits the people of three East African countries, either these three nations or some regional organization specific to this area should address the good's allocation. In some cases a regional network that connects nations confronting a common IPG issue needs to form, as in the case of river blindness. West African countries set up a network among themselves to control both the parasite worm and the person-to-person contagion of the disease. Other partners, such as Merck and donors, were included to provide financing and to make the drug Ivermectin available to curb the spread of the disease (Ferroni 2000, p. 17).

Subsidiarity not only places the problem on the most appropriate participants—those with the most at stake—but it also economizes on transaction cost. Focusing on the proper participants promotes allocative efficiency. The practice of subsidiarity involves a wide range of IPGs. For peacekeeping, NATO's assumption of missions in Bosnia and Kosovo made more sense than the UN being in charge, because instability in those countries poses a greater threat to NATO allies than to the world at large. Environmental treaties, such as the Helsinki Protocol to curb sulfur emissions in Europe, are best framed by the Europeans, which turned out to be the case.

Even many forms of foreign assistance involving IPGs can be improved by the subsidiarity principle where a cross-border spillover is handled by the agency whose geographical mandate is closest to the underlying IPG's range of spillovers. When the appropriate agency does not possess the requisite capacity, augmenting its capacity is better than assigning the problem to an organization with a larger geographical jurisdiction, unless economies of scale and scope warrant otherwise (Kanbur, Sandler, and Morrison 1999).[9] To put this recommendation into practice, the World Bank would have to increase the capacity of a host of regional banks and, in so doing, would be limiting its own capabilities.

SUPRANATIONAL INSTITUTIONS AND THEIR FINANCING

A variety of institutions within the international community provide a wide range of IPGs despite potential free-rider problems. Some institutions provide the necessary push or the lighter coax needed, while others operate as clubs. An examination of how these institutions succeed in financing their IPGs shows that the properties of the good, as well as other considerations discussed earlier, play a role in the design of these institutions. Table 4.3 lists the institutions covered along with a short institutional and financial description.

INTELSAT is a communications network that carries the majority of transoceanic messages. The system consists of 19 geostationary satellites positioned some 22,000 miles above the equator, from where the satellites orbit the earth in the same time interval that the earth rotates about its axis, thus leaving each satellite stationary over the earth. A mere three satellites are sufficient to provide point-to-multipoint service nearly anywhere on the planet. The other 16 satellites are used either to carry the volume of messages or serve as spares. Redundant backup satellites increase the system's reliability.

INTELSAT operates as a private consortium with firms, governments, and other institutions as members. Because coding and scrambling signals can restrict access to the network, INTELSAT qualifies as a club good. Use of the network can be finely monitored to a fraction of a second. As use of the communications system increases, the benefit per signal transmitted diminishes because of congestion in the form of interference when more signals share the same frequency bandwidth. Members are charged user fees or tolls based solely on their per unit use of the network. Everyone pays the same toll per unit of transmission, but total payments differ according to a member's total use. Voting at meetings of the board of governors, the supreme decisionmaking body of INTELSAT, is weighted according to members' use rates and investment shares. Such a voting scheme promotes optimality insofar as heavier users serve more individuals whose MWTP must be aggregated, and thus have a greater stake in provision and other policy decisions. INTELSAT's financial design is based on the benefit principle of equating the sum of MWTP to the marginal cost of provision through the use of tolls.

Although not listed in table 4.3, LANDSAT also operates as a privately owned club that charges users for remote sensing surveys of requested areas. Originally, LANDSAT was developed and funded by the U.S. government for military purposes, but was subsequently sold to private interests. A governmental boost was required because of high research and development costs and the expense of lifting satellites into orbit. LANDSAT thus represents a case where a government provided the club with an initial provision and development push, and then allowed the private sector to take over. Other international club goods

Table 4.3. Examples of Supranational Institutions and Their Financing Arrangements

Institution	Institutional description	Financial arrangement
INTELSAT	A communication satellite network with countries and firms as members of a consortium. Satellites positioned in geostationary space provide global communication.	Operates as a club with charges to members based on tolls taking account of congestion. Total tolls differ based on total utilization.
UN peacekeeping	Since 1975, countries have been assessed shares to support each operation. Voting privilege in the General Assembly can be suspended for a nonpayer if assessments are too far in arrears.	Countries are distinguished by four categories based on ability to pay (horizontal and vertical equity) and benefit principle. Strong vertical equity considerations dominate.
UN	The UN provides a host of GPGs and IPGs through its regular membership fees and members' voluntary contributions. These public goods differ according to exclusion, nonrivalry, and joint products. Economies of scope are being exploited.	Financing is based on ability to pay with a strong emphasis on vertical equity and UN status. Less vertical equity than peacekeeping assessments. Voluntary contributions are a small part of funding.
NATO	An alliance established in 1949 that has grown from 12 to 19 allies. Article 5 indicates that an attack on one ally will be viewed as an attack on all allies. Mission has changed numerous times and now involves crisis management and nonproliferation of weapons of mass destruction. Multiple public goods provided to exploit economies of scope.	Most (99.5 percent) of allies' expenditures on defense are done independently, with only 0.5 percent done commonly to maintain infrastructure, NATO civil structure, and NATO military command. Defense spending appears to be based on the benefit principle because of the high ratio of excludable benefits.
WHO	Mission is to pursue the maintenance of world health. Part of the UN. Joint products are present.	Based on membership assessments, and thus on ability to pay. Also based on donated trust funds for specific purposes.

(Table continues on the following page.)

Table 4.3. (*continued*)

Institution	Institutional description	Financial arrangement
Environmental treaties	Agreements to curb various pollutants, including CFCs, sulfur, nitrogen oxides, and greenhouse gases.	Montreal Protocol on CFCs relies on a multilateral fund with contributions based on ability to pay. Most treaties depend on members financing their own cutbacks based on the benefit principle.
EU	Economic union to eliminate trade and nontrade barriers among members. The EU pursues the free movement of goods, services, people, and capital. Public good of trade creation within union and gains in efficiency (that is, specialization of labor, economies of scale, and growth). A host of other public goods of varying purity and joint products, for example, security, traffic control, contract conventions, and health standards. Also income redistribution practiced. Economies of scope are being exploited.	Value added taxes on exchanges within the EU are used to finance public goods and infrastructure linking EU members. Taxation abides by ability to pay rather than benefit principle. Significant redistribution and inefficiency tied to the Common Agricultural Policy.
World Bank	A multilateral agency providing development assistance, technical advice, and research findings. It also coordinates development assistance from other donors, for instance, nongovernmental organizations and bilateral donors. The Bank's activities vary in their degree of publicness and the presence of joint products. Alleviation of poverty with little or no conditionality has a large share of purely public benefits. The Bank's research outputs possess mostly purely public benefits.	Financing for the Bank's activities comes from member countries' subscriptions to the capital stock. Country-specific inducements for subscribing derive, in part, from its number of votes, which is based directly on its subscription. Larger subscribers obtain a greater number and, thus, a larger share of votes on Bank's policies.

IMO	For international shipping, the IMO oversees international trade and institutes conventions on accidents and accident prevention, innocent passage, pollution, and other concerns.	The IMO is a specialized UN agency financed through membership fees. Nations willing to sacrifice autonomy to achieve coordination and the public good of safety that results.
ITU	The ITU establishes practices to curb signal interference and allocates the frequency bands of the electromagnetic spectrum to purposes and countries. Promotes adoption of standardized equipment.	The ITU is a specialized UN agency financed through membership fees. In nations' interests to achieve cooperation.
Medicines for Malaria Venture	A joint public-private partnership to control malaria that involves WHO, the World Bank, the Rockefeller Foundation, the United States, the International Federation of Pharmaceutical Manufacturers Association, and the Association of British Pharmaceutical Industries. Aim is to discover and develop new drugs to treat and prevent malaria.	Funding comes from multilateral agencies, donor countries, nonprofits, foundations, and nongovernmental organizations. Some pharmaceutical firms will partner drug discovery projects by lending their expertise and facilities. The venture will approach industrial partners to manufacture and market newly discovered and effective drugs. High-risk activity of discovery being collectively funded by multilaterals and other donors. Pooling of efforts to achieve best shot discovery.
Onchocerciasis Control Program	In operation in West Africa for more than 25 years to control river blindness, a condition caused by a parasitic worm. Partners include multilaterals, Merck Corporation, African governments, local communities, bilateral donors, foundations, and nongovernmental organizations. Exploit participants' comparative advantages.	Funding supplied by the various participants, with Merck making Ivermectin available for free. Control of river blindness and its contagion is an example of a weakest link public good.

Source: Medicines for Malaria Venture and Onchocerciasis Control Program: Ferroni (2000, pp. 10, 17); see the text for other sources.

include the Suez and Panama canals, which charge tolls per transit. Internet providers constitute another instance of a club where members are charged for their use of the network, and proceeds fund increases in the providers' server capacity and reliability. Such increases help to limit congestion in the form of connecting and waiting time.

UN peacekeeping efforts involve peacekeeping, peace enforcement (when the two sides do not agree to be separated), and humanitarian relief efforts (see Sandler and Hartley 1999, chapter 4; 2001 on UN peacekeeping and its financial arrangements). Following the UN's first sizable operation in the former Belgian Congo during 1960–64, it became apparent that UN resources would be stretched too thinly if such operations were funded from regular membership fees, as originally planned. Given the public nature of peacekeeping, early attempts to solicit voluntary contributions yielded little funding. To create a more permanent and reliable funding source, the UN General Assembly passed a resolution that established assessment accounts for peacekeeping operations, beginning in 1975.

These assessment accounts distinguished 4 classes of payers: the 5 permanent members of the Security Council (class A), 22 industrial countries that are not permanent members of the council (class B), wealthy developing countries (class C), and poorer developing countries (class D). Nations in classes A and B finance the lion's share of peacekeeping operations, with permanent members of the Security Council paying 63 percent and industrial nations in class B paying almost 35 percent, on average. Thus countries in classes C and D underwrite just 2 percent of peacekeeping operations. The five countries in class A pay 22 percent more than their regular budget assessment scale to peacekeeping. Thus the United States covers 25 percent of the UN's regular budget, but it must fund approximately 31 percent of peacekeeping expenses. Class B nations pay their regular budget assessment scale, class C countries pay 1/5th of their regular budget assessment scale, and class D countries pay 1/10th of their regular budget assessment scale. Assessed peacekeeping burdens are intended to be disproportionate in terms of income and, as such, display strong ability to pay equity considerations. Because nations within designated classes are treated identically, horizontal equity is also practiced.

Once a UN member is in arrears for its assessed amounts for two full preceding years, Article 19 of the UN Charter provides that the member can lose its voting privilege in the General Assembly. For class A members, this penalty is not as severe as losing its vote on the Security Council. Because council members, and wealthy nations in general, have a greater interest in peacekeeping, the assessment accounts also apply the benefit principle to a small extent. Clearly, however, the strong elements of nonrivalry, nonexcludability, and best shot aggregation mean that a supranational institution is required to provide the push.

The UN is one of the most complex supranational institutions shown in table 4.3, and serves as the umbrella organization for smaller, specialized agencies that are financed through membership fees, donated trust funds, and UN support, for instance, WHO and the IMO. The UN provides a host of IPGs, financed through regular membership fees and voluntary contributions. (Although voluntary contributions are a source of funding, such contributions represent an extremely small share of UN total financing.) The UN supplies numerous IPGs so as to take advantage of economies of scope stemming from common elements of its massive infrastructure, which can economize on cost. Regular membership assessment is guided primarily by ability to pay considerations that stress less vertical equity than was true for peacekeeping assessment accounts. Assessment scales are altered periodically to adjust for member nations' changing economic fortunes in terms of income. For example, Russia's membership assessment scale has been reduced since the breakup of the Soviet Union, as the Russian economy has shrunk, while Japan's assessment scale has been increased. In its role of supplying information, the UN charges for its print and electronic publications, and in so doing uses exclusion of impure public goods as a way to establish a market in information. Given the vast array of public goods supported by the UN and its subsidiary organizations, the use of a variety of financial instruments, guided by the goods' three dimensions of publicness, is not surprising. Supplemental support from regular membership fees or specific assessments is required to finance nonrival and nonexcludable benefits where user fees are not feasible.

NATO is a military alliance that shares deterrence coming from a collective threat of punishment to any state attacking the territory or the interests of a member ally. Established in 1949, NATO has grown from its 12 original allies to 19. Allies share a defense activity that yields joint products that vary in their degree of publicness (Sandler and Hartley 2001). An arsenal may deter aggression while allowing the provider to pursue its own territorial ambitions, where deterrence and imperialism are the joint products. An alliance can fulfill at least three general functions: (a) deterrence, (b) damage limitation or protection, and (c) private or ally-specific benefits. Deterrence is purely public among the allies and the most subject to free-riding concerns. In contrast, damage-limiting protection, needed when deterrence fails and war ensues, is subject to rivalry in the form of force thinning as a given contingent of forces is spread to defend a longer exposed border. Private or ally-specific benefits occur when a jointly produced defense output assists the provider, but the output's benefits are not available to others. Such private benefits include quelling domestic unrest, controlling domestic terrorism, responding to national disasters, or patrolling coastal waters.

As the share of excludable to total defense benefits increases, an alliance can rely on allies' independent behavior to spend where their benefits are the greatest. Sandler and Hartley (1999, 2001) argue that from the 1970s until the present day, a sizable portion of defense benefits is excludable, so that the benefit principle can be partly satisfied by independent spending decisions. In practice, NATO allies do make independent spending choices. Less than 1 percent of its allies' aggregate expenditures on defense are used to commonly fund NATO's civil structure, infrastructure, and integrated military command, so that more than 99 percent is spent independently by the allies. Over the years as weapons technology, the strategic mission, membership composition, and threats have evolved, the mix of joint products, and thus the ratio of excludable benefits, has also changed. As these changes occur, financial arrangements need adjusting: as this ratio increases or decreases, there is less or more of a need for explicit coordination among allies. Recent changes in NATO's strategic mission, which stresses peacekeeping and nonproliferation of weapons of mass destruction, have decreased the ratio of excludable benefits, thereby calling into question the wisdom of NATO's loose structure. As mentioned earlier, NATO's provision of multiple public goods indicates that it is exploiting economies of scope.

WHO's mission is the maintenance of world health, which has both country-specific and worldwide public benefits. WHO provides services to member governments in the form of expert guidance, practical projects, health manpower training, and health program coordination. By coordinating health programs internationally, WHO aims to foster a network of transnational cooperation in health practices. Such a network is expected to give rise to some purely public benefits as intelligence on diseases and epidemics is shared and best practices are disseminated. Clearly, country-specific benefits derive from projects and health manpower training, whereas some rivalry results from expert guidance as a fixed number of staff must cover more countries. Given the presence of joint products, WHO could be funded by a combination of user fees and fixed membership charges, with the former covering excludable benefits and the latter charging for the nonexcludable benefits. In practice, however, WHO is a specialized UN agency supported by membership fees based on ability to pay and donated trust funds earmarked for specific purposes.

Recent years have seen a number of transnational environmental treaties to curb CFCs, sulfur, nitrogen oxides, and other pollutants (Sandler 1997). Most treaties rely on the signers to fulfill pledged cutbacks. At the international level, the UN Environment Programme, supported by UN membership fees, supplies the minimal infrastructure in terms of making treaty text available and collecting the signatures of ratifying countries. Through its ability to pay membership charge, the UN supports this purely public benefit. The Montreal Protocol on stratospheric ozone depleting substances provides for a multilateral trust fund to help developing countries acquire the technology to substitute more ozone-friendly substitutes. Not surprisingly, this fund for what amounts to a pure public good is provided by contributions on behalf of just the rich countries and is rather modest in size. Thus an official push is needed and received from leader nations. For most treaties, significant country-specific benefits arising from either joint products or a weighted sum technology induce ratifiers to finance their own cutbacks and, in so doing, respond to benefits received.

The EU was originally established to eliminate trade and nontrade barriers among members by pursuing the free flow of goods, services, people, and capital. In its trade creation role, the EU provides a pure IPG to its member states by increasing welfare through static and dynamic efficiency gains from enhanced specialization of labor and scale economies resulting from the increased size of the market. Over the years the EU has evolved from its common market purpose and assumed the provision of additional public goods, for example, security, traffic control, contract standardization, health standards, pollution cleanup, monetary union, and scientific discoveries. As such, the EU is another instance where multiple public goods are provided to exploit economies of scope. These IPGs vary in their characteristics, for instance, contract standardization represents a best shot IPG abiding by a coordination game.

The EU is unique among supranational structures in the grandeur of its vision (ideally, to create a United States of Europe) and design. At least three features set the EU apart from other supranational institutions: (a) the use of a value added tax on EU exchanges, (b) the Common Agricultural Policy, and (c) its efforts to redistribute income from rich to poor nations. The value added taxes on consumption not only finance the provision of public goods by the EU, but they also underwrite efforts to redistribute income among member states. Infrastructure projects have been specifically placed in poorer member countries to provide public goods while giving such members an income transfer. Value added consumption taxes are more in keeping with an ability to pay rather than a benefit principle of taxation. The Common Agricultural Policy has diverted trade, added to inefficiency, and caused significant redistributions within and among member countries' farm populations. The EU's frequent crises illustrate that even nations with much in common resist sacrificing autonomy on monetary, fiscal, and tax policies.

The World Bank is a multilateral agency that provides IPGs in the form of development assistance, technical advice, and research findings. In addition, the Bank coordinates development assistance from a host of donors, including nongovernmental organizations, countries, and charitable foundations. The Bank's activities vary in their public characteristics and the presence of joint products. Some activities—unconditional poverty alleviation and basic research—are primarily purely public among members, while other activities—fostering environmental quality and limiting migration—are apt to have the greatest impact on host and neighboring countries.

The World Bank is financed by member countries' subscriptions to its capital stock, used for loans and to support the Bank's activities. An important country-specific benefit is promoted by assigning a member's votes in the Bank based on the size of its subscription (World Bank 1999). In 1999 the United States held more than 16 percent of the votes on the Bank's policies because of its generous subscription. Thus in return for carrying a greater burden of World Bank financing, a large subscriber gains greater autonomy over the Bank's policy decisions and direction. This support for votes practice provides a significant member-specific inducement that helps circumvent the free-rider problem. The International Monetary Fund implements a similar policy. Institutional design can provide joint products and promote incentives. This assignment of vote shares stand in stark contrast to a nation's single vote in the UN General Assembly regardless of the UN financial burden that a member carries.

The IMO and the ITU are specialized UN agencies that oversee international shipping and communication, respectively. Membership fees that nations willingly pay finance both the IMO and the ITU. International trade and communications networks must address a number of collective action issues of a weakest link or best shot nature: interoperability or interconnectedness, accidents and mishaps, jurisdictional rights, and competitive practices (Zacher and Sutton 1996). For international shipping, the IMO institutes conventions on accidents and accident prevention, innocent passage, pollution, and other concerns. For telecommunications, the ITU establishes practices to curb signal interference and allocates the frequency bands of the electromagnetic spectrum to various specific purposes. The ITU also promotes the adoption of standardized equipment. A significant factor inducing nations to join these international institutions and to submit to their regulations involves mutual self-interest in achieving the free flow of trade and communication among nations. Even though nations must sacrifice some autonomy over commerce and communications by satisfying these regulations, the true loss of autonomy is modest, meaning that the gain from standardized practices does not have to be great to still provide each nation with a net gain over membership fees. Safety at sea and/or freedom from interference along the spectrum represents a weakest link public good, whose outcome is determined by the least careful behavior of the participants. In general, the adoption of standards of behavior or safety conventions denotes a best shot IPG and adheres to a coordination game structure, where it is in the interests of each nation to abide by the agreed upon conventions and to pay membership fees to support the institutions creating such conventions. A nation that defects from a standard is significantly worse off if the others continue to abide by it.

The Medicines for Malaria Venture and the Onchocerciasis Control Program represent joint public-private partnerships (Ferroni 2000). The Medicines for Malaria Venture involves a partnership that includes WHO, the World Bank, the Rockefeller Foundation, the United States, and two associations of pharmaceutical companies. This partnership is fused together to focus resources sufficiently to achieve best shot IPGs of discovering new medicines. By forming this partnership, each participant is asked to make a relatively modest donation to a team in contrast to the amount that would be involved if a participant had to go it alone. In the case of the Onchocerciasis Control Program the partnership provides a weakest link public good, where incentives are right for the African governments to match one another's contributions. For both cases, partnerships can provide the necessary funding because of the supportive incentive structure associated with the underlying IPGs' aggregation technology.

The design of these organizations illustrates some common themes that underscore the importance of the earlier theoretical discussion. First, if exclusion is feasible and use can be monitored, then private provision can be financed through a club arrangement. Second, when a public sector push is required in the form of a supranational organization, multiple public goods are frequently provided because of economies of scope. Many elaborate supranational institutions address a number of IPG problems. Third, when a push is required, supranational structures rely on ability to pay instruments to fund IPGs, and thus sacrifice efficiency for feasibility. Fourth, with joint products, more of a coax than a push is provided by the supranational structure, as country-specific and club benefits motivate contributions. Such structures can remain loose with modest common financing and enforcement efforts, for example, NATO and environmental treaties. Fifth, if a push is required for weakest link and best shot IPGs, then a partnership among private and public participants may coalesce resources so that either a minimally acceptable level is supplied by all or the required threshold for success is achieved.

CONCLUSIONS

Not all IPGs are created equal. The three dimensions of these goods— nonrivalry of benefits, excludability possibilities, and aggregation technology—determine what kinds of institutions or transnational actions are required to provide and finance them. For purely and impurely public goods where exclusion of nonpayers is not feasible, a real push is needed by the international community to provide these goods. A supranational structure is then required to institute membership fees or taxes to underwrite the IPGs. For weakest link and/or best shot IPGs, partnerships among public and private institutions can either ensure that everyone meets acceptable levels of a weakest link IPG or that sufficient resources are accumulated to support a best shot IPG. When club goods are present, users can form private collectives and fully finance the shared good with congestion tolls under a variety of scenarios, depending on production considerations, the nature of crowding, and competitive conditions. For activities giving rise to joint products, only a little coaxing from the international community is necessary if a large share of country-specific benefits exists or is complementary to the jointly produced public benefits. The basic message is simple: financing does not pose insurmountable problems for many IPGs. As researchers gain a better appreciation of how the nature of IPGs differs, they will acquire insights about the proper actions to support IPGs. The transnational community should only explicitly direct scarce resources to those IPGs that need a significant push or a smaller coax. When clubs or markets can finance IPGs, the transnational community should sit back and let incentives guide the actions of sovereign nations.

NOTES

1. Two recent books (Kaul, Grunberg, and Sandler 1999; Sandler 1997) discuss the connection between IPGs and global contingencies (for example, global warming) confronting humankind. See also Kanbur, Sandler, and Morrison (1999) and Sandler (1998).

2. Technological advances create goods whose benefits extend beyond the providing nation, for example, hydrofluorocarbons, which are new refrigerants without ozone destroying side effects. Technology also increases digital-based communication, and thus the spread of knowledge via optical cables and satellite links. This not only serves as an intermediate input for IPGs, but also enhances the demand for these goods. Furthermore, digital technologies foster the universality of knowledge, and in some instances help support a property rights regime for the distribution of IPGs.

3. This chapter does not address how the international community prioritizes among alternative IPGs, except to note that ideally this should hinge on the sum of the associated marginal willingness to pay (Cornes and Sandler 1996, chapter 6) and marginal cost of provision.

4. If neutrality applies, then collective provision can reduce private provision, and can result in no increase in the overall level of the public good. However, neutrality does not result in a smaller overall level of the public good.

5. Clubs involve at least two allocative choices: the provision level and the membership size. The choice of the toll fixes the membership size. These two decisions are interdependent and must be made simultaneously.

6. With a homogeneous of degree zero congestion function, any increase in crowding from further utilization just offsets the decrease in crowding from greater provision, because utilization and provision increase proportionally (Cornes and Sandler 1996, pp. 272–77, 391–93).

7. The first treatment of alternative aggregate technologies is by Hirshleifer (1983), who refers to them as the social composition function. Arce and Sandler (2001), Cornes (1993), Sandler (1992), Sandler and Sargent (1995), Vicary (1990), and Vicary and Sandler (forthcoming) analyze numerous aggregation technologies. In a foreign assistance context, Ferroni (2000); Jayaraman and Kanbur (1999); and Kanbur, Sandler, and Morrison (1999) address the importance of alternative aggregation technologies.

8. Assurance games are a special subclass of coordination games. On the strategic implications associated with weaker link public goods see Arce and Sandler (2001). For weaker link public goods the smallest contribution has the largest marginal influence on utility, followed by the second smallest contribution, and so on. See also Cornes (1993).

9. The existence of economies of scope clashes with an ideal notion of subsidiarity. A framework for subsidiarity that acknowledges economies of scale and economies of scope needs to be formulated.

REFERENCES

Arce M., Daniel G., and Todd Sandler. 2001. "Transnational Public Goods: Strategies and Institutions." *European Journal of Political Economy* 17(3): 493–516.

Bruce, Neil. 1998. *Public Finance and the American Economy*. Reading, Massachusetts: Addison-Wesley.

Buchanan, James M. 1965. "An Economic Theory of Clubs." *Economica* 32(1): 1–14.

Buchholz, Wolfgang, and Kai A. Konrad. 1995. "Strategic Transfers and Private Provision of Public Goods." *Journal of Public Economics* 57(3): 489–505.

Buchholz, Wolfgang, Christian Haslbeck, and Todd Sandler. 1998. "When Does Partial Cooperation Pay?" *Finanzarchiv* 55(1): 1–20.

Cornes, Richard. 1993. "Dyke Maintenance and Other Stories: Some Neglected Types of Public Goods." *Quarterly Journal of Economics* 108(1): 259–71.

Cornes, Richard, and Todd Sandler. 1996. *The Theory of Externalities, Public Goods, and Club Goods*, 2nd ed. Cambridge, U.K.: Cambridge University Press.

DeSerpa, Allan C. 1978. "Congestion, Pollution, and Impure Public Goods." *Public Finance* 33(1–2): 68–83.

Ferroni, Marco. 2000. "Reforming Foreign Aid: The Role of International Public Goods." Operations Evaluation Department Working Paper Series no. 4. World Bank, Washington, D.C.

Heckathorn, Douglas D. 1989. "Collective Action and the Second-Order Free-Rider Problem." *Rationality and Society* 1(1): 78–100.

Hirshleifer, Jack. 1983. "From Weakest-Link to Best Shot: The Voluntary Provision of Public Goods." *Public Choice* 41(3): 371–86.

Jayaraman, Rajshri, and Ravi Kanbur. 1999. "International Public Goods and the Case for Foreign Aid." In Inge Kaul, Isabelle Grunberg, and Marc A. Stern, eds., *Global Public Goods: International Cooperation in the 21st Century*. New York: Oxford University Press.

Kanbur, Ravi, Todd Sandler, with Kevin Morrison. 1999. *The Future of Development Assistance: Common Pools and International Public Goods*. Policy Essay no. 25. Washington, D.C.: Overseas Development Council.

Kaul, Inge, Isabelle Grunberg, and Marc A. Stern, eds. 1999. *Global Public Goods: International Cooperation in the 21st Century*. New York: Oxford University Press.

Murdoch, James C., Todd Sandler, and Keith Sargent. 1997. "A Tale of Two Collectives: Sulphur versus Nitrogen Oxides Emission Reduction in Europe." *Economica* 64(2): 281–301.

Oakland, William. 1972. "Congestion, Public Goods, and Welfare." *Journal of Public Economics* 1(3–4): 339–57.

Olson, Mancur. 1965. *The Logic of Collective Action*. Cambridge, Massachusetts: Harvard University Press.

———. 1969. "The Principle of 'Fiscal Equivalence': The Division of Responsibilities among Different Levels of Government." *American Economics Review Papers and Proceedings* 59(2): 479–87.

Sandler, Todd. 1977. "Impurity of Defense: An Application to the Economics of Alliances." *KYKLOS* 30(3): 443–60.

———. 1992. *Collective Action: Theory and Applications*. Ann Arbor, Michigan: University of Michigan Press.

———. 1997. *Global Challenges: An Approach to Environmental, Political, and Economic Problems*. Cambridge, U.K.: Cambridge University Press.

————. 1998. "Global and Regional Public Goods: A Prognosis for Collective Action." *Fiscal Studies* 19(3): 221–47.

————. 1999. "Intergenerational Public Goods: Strategies, Efficiency, and Institutions." In Inge Kaul, Isabelle Grunberg, and Marc A. Stern, eds., *Global Public Goods: International Cooperation in the 21st Century.* New York: Oxford University Press.

Sandler, Todd, and Keith Hartley. 1999. *The Political Economy of NATO: Past, Present, and into the 21st Century.* Cambridge, U.K.: Cambridge University Press.

————. 2001. "Economics of Alliance: The Lessons for Collective Action." *Journal of Economic Literature* 39(3): 869–96.

Sandler, Todd, and Keith Sargent. 1995. "Management of Transnational Commons: Coordination, Publicness, and Treaty Formation." *Land Economics* 71(2): 145–62.

Sandler, Todd, and John T. Tschirhart. 1997. "Club Theory: Thirty Years Later." *Public Choice* 93(3–4): 335–55.

Siqueira, Kevin, and Todd Sandler. 2001. "Models of Alliances: Internalizing Externalities and Financing." *Defence and Peace Economics* 12(3): 249–70.

Small, Kenneth A. 1999. "Economies of Scale and Self-Financing Rules with Noncompetitive Factor Markets." *Journal of Public Economics* 74(3): 431–50.

Vicary, Simon. 1990. "Transfers and the Weakest Link: An Extension of Hirshleifer's Analysis." *Journal of Public Economics* 43(3): 375–94.

Vicary, Simon, and Todd Sandler. Forthcoming. "Weakest-Link Public Goods: Giving In-Kind or Transferring Money." *European Economic Review.*

Warr, Peter G. 1983. "The Private Provision of a Public Good Is Independent of the Distribution of Income." *Economics Letters* 13(2): 207–11.

World Bank. 1999. *International Bank for Reconstruction and Development: Financial Statements, June 30, 1999.* Washington, D.C.: World Bank. Available on: www.worldbank.org/html/extpb/annrep99.

Zacher, Mark A., with Brent A. Sutton. 1996. *Governing Global Networks: International Regimes for Transportation and Communications.* Cambridge, U.K.: Cambridge University Press.

Chapter 5

ALLOCATING AID TO INTERNATIONAL PUBLIC GOODS

Dirk Willem te Velde, Oliver Morrissey, and Adrian Hewitt

Although discussion of international public goods (IPGs) and the need to finance them is of fairly recent vintage, donors have been granting aid, or official development assistance (ODA), in substantial quantities for many decades, and have always allocated some of this aid to financing public goods. IPGs have not suddenly appeared. International agricultural research and research on disease eradication, for example, have a long history and both have been financially supported by aid from donors.

This chapter, which is based on more detailed results reported in Hewitt, Morrissey, and te Velde (2001, available from the authors on request), asks two questions. First, how much aid has been allocated to finance what would now be classified as public goods, especially IPGs? Second, has the increasing prominence of IPGs (for example, as new diseases such as AIDS emerge or as countries perceive global warming as a problem) increased the share of aid allocated to public goods, and has total aid spending been affected? This chapter addresses these questions by examining a breakdown of aid spending by type of public good, by sector, and by donor agency.

Chapter 2 focused on classifying public goods, concentrating on two types. First, it distinguished between international and national public goods (NPGs). Second, it distinguished between core activities and complementary activities (World Bank 2001). Although almost all core activities are international in their spillover range, NPGs tend to be complementary to the provision of IPGs.

The specific aim of this chapter is to quantify how much donor aid during 1980–98 financed the provision of public goods in developing countries.

Significant financing of IPG provision does not take place in developing countries, and hence is not financed out of aid expenditures. For example, much funding for medical research, which contributes knowledge to provide health IPGs, is within the rich countries. Similarly, much of the funding for the costs of running global institutions that are a component of providing IPGs, such as the United Nations (UN) system or the World Trade Organization, is not considered part of aid. Consequently, our analysis does not capture a significant portion of global funding for providing IPGs. In addition, our figures do not reflect governments' own funding of national public goods in developing countries.

The measure of aid we use is aid commitments from the Creditor Reporting System (CRS) of the Development Assistance Committee (DAC) of the Organisation for Economic Co-operation and Development (OECD). Previous empirical analyses using DAC-CRS data have examined aid spending on total IPGs (for example, Raffer 1998) or on total IPGs by sector (World Bank 2001). Our estimates cover aid spending on public goods (national and international) in total and by sector, and we also consider the allocation by individual donors (the 19 major DAC bilateral donors and the 6 multilateral donors). For the bilateral donors we consider aid allocated to public goods provision both as a share of aid and as a share of donor gross domestic product (GDP). The results reveal significant differences in the emphasis different donors attach to supporting the provision of various categories of public goods in developing countries.

Our principal conclusions are as follows. First, the share of public goods spending in aid budgets has increased steadily over the last two decades. Second, in the 1980s, this increase was accompanied by an increase in the overall level of aid. While aid levels fell in the1990s, the share of public goods in aid continued to rise, suggesting a displacement of other aid. Third, donors with large aid budgets tend to be those that also have a large share of IPGs in their aid portfolios, although during the 1990s, almost all donors increased their share of IPGs.

CLASSIFYING AID FOR NATIONAL AND INTERNATIONAL PUBLIC GOODS

As discussed in chapter 2, the issue of the spillover range—over what geographical range does the good have the features of "publicness"—is an important element in the operationalization of the concept of public goods. Kanbur,

Sandler, and Morrison (1999) distinguish three types of spillover range: national, regional, and global. These distinctions are not always precise, and our working definition (following chapter 2) is as follows. In the case of an IPG, once the good has been provided, its benefits or associated externalities spill across national boundaries and are potentially globally nonrival and nonexcludable. In contrast, once an NPG has been provided, the benefits accrue largely, if not entirely, to residents of the country in question.

As in chapter 2, we distinguish between five different "sectors" of IPGs (and NPGs). The best known examples of IPGs often relate to the environment (E) and health (H), and recently the literature has given considerable attention to peacekeeping or conflict prevention (P) and knowledge generation (K). There is less agreement regarding the extent to which economic and financial governance (G) is indeed a global public good. Following chapter 2, we treat governance as essentially a complementary activity that is national in range. This is dictated, in part, by our focus on aid that is committed to specific countries, leading to the omission of global governance institutions, which would more appropriately be classified as IPGs.

Environment (E)

Global warming and climate change have highlighted the global public nature of environmental goods. Environmental policy and education and protection of the biosphere (reduction of greenhouse gas emissions) are of global relevance. Local environmental projects often relate to issues of global concern and have cross-boundary spillovers, and hence are treated as IPGs. Examples of such projects include protection of biodiversity, World Heritage sites, or rain forests and reduction of pollution emissions such as effluent into water or toxic waste (thus waste management is included). Many environmental projects have significant regional, and possibly even global, effects, for example, river and water resources management, fisheries, and forestry policy. All these are included as IPGs. One could argue that research into alternative energy sources, such as solar or wind power, provides for an IPG in that it ultimately contributes to reduced greenhouse gas emissions; however, we classify projects on alternative energy sources as NPGs, on the basis that they contribute to national capacity to produce energy without increasing (rather than actually reducing) emissions. In this sense they are complementary production activities. While the research would be an IPG, we treat energy projects as NPGs. Similarly, we treat agricultural and land use projects as NPGs, along with housing policy, which can contribute to the urban environment.

Health (H)

The provision of general health care is an NPG or complementary activity, because improving a population's health involves significant externalities. However, certain expenditures, such as eradicating communicable diseases, relate to IPGs. Aid funds have supported expenditures to control infectious diseases, including HIV/AIDS. The literature often treats family planning and population control as IPGs, because rapid population growth creates environmental stress with potential global effects, and because of the existence of bodies such as the United Nations Population Fund that coordinate global policy. However, we treat all such categories as NPGs, because the benefits are largely national and complementary to the core activity. Similarly, sanitation, improved water supply, and social services all improve the health environment in which people live, thereby contributing to welfare and reducing the spread of disease, and we classify them as NPGs.

Knowledge (K)

Education provision is a basic NPG, and is essential if a country is to be able to participate in global knowledge, that is, to benefit from knowledge IPGs. Basic education is an important complementary activity. Global knowledge management initiatives in different fields—such as technical assistance to provide hardware and software for Internet connections—constitute core activities and we classify them as IPGs. International agricultural research centers provide an IPG, and expenditure on international agricultural research is included under K to capture such spending, but will not capture all spending on international agricultural research centers. Projects for technology research and to build research capacity are also included, as are measures to increase global dissemination of, and participation in, knowledge, for instance, *Infodev* (see http://www.infodev.org/) and the African Virtual University.

Economic and Financial Governance (G)

As discussed in chapter 2, the economic and financial governance sector is not easily reconciled with the notion of public goods. Building governance capacity, such as legal systems and civil society, especially in the context of economic policy and management, confers public benefits and is classed as an NPG. Financing specifically allocated to support regional initiatives, such as economic integration, or participation in global forums, for example, technical assistance for members of the World Trade Organization, could be defined as IPGs. Unfortunately, such expenditures are not separately identified in the CRS data.

Conflict Prevention and Postconflict Assistance with a Multicountry Scope (P)

Expenditures on preventing or alleviating the effects of conflict are IPGs in that they provide regional security benefits. Even if the global benefit is limited, there are clearly international benefits. This can include peacekeeping in developing countries. Postconflict reconstruction and mine clearing are more properly treated as NPGs, as is support for elections and human rights. We exclude food aid, help for refugees, and emergency relief from either category of public good, as these are private in nature.

Classifying Aid Allocations to Public Goods

As noted, like similar exercises (Raffer 1998; World Bank 2001), we use the CRS as our data source. The CRS is the main source of statistics on the sectoral and geographical distribution of aid. One disadvantage of this database, and indeed of most databases on aid, is that it does not distinguish between aid contributing to the financing of IPGs and aid contributing to non-IPGs, nor does it distinguish aid for projects with multicountry benefits. Furthermore, as mentioned earlier, aid allocations capture only part of donor countries' spending on IPG provision. The coverage of multilateral donors in the CRS is incomplete, and may even exclude some of their aid spending on IPGs, for example, by the World Bank using trust funds. Another disadvantage is that the CRS relates to aid commitments rather than disbursements, and hence may not relate to actual expenditures. Nevertheless, it provides a good indication of donor's intended aid allocation by sector.

The CRS data on aid commitments list projects according to a five-digit classification scheme (see appendix 5A for the allocation of aid to IPGs and NPGs by sector according to CRS codes). We recognize that this classification scheme is sometimes not sufficiently detailed to make a decision about the inclusion of a specific CRS item into an IPG category. Specifically, some judgments must be made in distinguishing between NPGs and IPGs. We adopt a reasonably strict definition of IPGs, but a somewhat more generous definition of NPGs. The classification in this chapter is similar to that in World Bank (2001); appendix 5B details the principal differences.

AID FINANCING OF PUBLIC GOODS BY SECTOR AND DONOR, 1980–98

For the empirical analysis reported here, ODA commitments (from CRS data) are allocated to the IPG and NPG sectors identified earlier. The data cover 19 bilateral donors and 6 multilateral donors. Allocations were calculated as the average over three years for four periods: 1980–82, 1985–87, 1990–92, and 1996–98. This allows us to examine how spending on IPGs and NPGs, and on which sectors, has evolved over time. The allocations are measured in value terms (U.S. dollars in current prices), as a percentage of total ODA, and as a percentage of GDP for all donors.

In overall value terms, donors spent some US$340 million per year on IPGs in the early 1980s, rising to about US$1.3 billion per year in the late 1990s. The corresponding figures for NPGs were US$800 million and US$4.5 billion, respectively.[1] During the same period the value of global aid roughly doubled and world GDP roughly trebled. Clearly, the real and relative value of aid spending on public goods increased.

In sector terms, for IPGs most spending was on the environment (E-IPGs) during all four periods, although the greatest increase in spending between 1980 and 1998 was on health (H-IPGs). Similarly, for NPGs the environment (E-NPGs) accounted for the most spending during each period, although spending on government services (G-NPGs) increased the most. The donors spending the most on IPGs in the early 1980s were the International Development Association (IDA, the World Bank window for concessional lending), Japan, Germany, the European Union, and Sweden. By the late 1990s the top five in value terms were Japan, IDA, the United States, France, and the Netherlands. However, looking at absolute values is not as revealing as looking at spending relative to aid and to donors' GDP.

Share of Aid Allocated to Public Goods

Relative to total aid spending by all DAC donors, IPGs accounted for nearly 5 percent in 1980–82, almost 7 percent in 1990–92, and close to 9 percent in 1996–98 (table 5.1). These shares are slightly different from those in World Bank (2001), although the pattern over time is similar. Both estimates indicate an increase in the early to mid-1990s that continued into the mid-1990s before stabilizing, and possibly even declining somewhat in the late 1990s. This may suggest that spending on IPGs was given a boost in the post-Cold War period. Whether this new level is temporary or whether a further rise or fall will occur remains to be seen.

The increase in aid allocated to NPGs was fairly evenly spread over the period, with some acceleration in the early 1990s (table 5.2). Total expenditure on NPGs by DAC donors rose from just over 11 percent of aid in 1980–82, to more than 21 percent in the early 1990s, reaching almost 30 percent in 1996–98.

Thus, taken together, more than 16 percent of all aid was allocated to financing public goods in the early 1980s, but by the late 1990s the proportion had risen to almost 39 percent (table 5.3).

Because the demarcation between national and international public goods is not a precise one, people could differ in their views of how much aid really finances IPGs. Our estimates suggest that more than 10 cents of every dollar of aid go to IPGs. If one believes that NPG spillovers are significant and should be attributed to IPGs, or if one wishes to include action on debt, then the financing of IPGs could account for about a fifth of all aid flows.[2] As discussed later, CRS data could significantly underestimate donor spending on IPGs in developing countries. Thus concluding that currently some 15 to 20 percent of aid finances the provision of IPGs in developing countries may be fair.

Table 5.1. Spending on International Public Goods as a Percentage of Aid, Selected Years, 1980–98

Donor	1980–82	1990–92	1996–98
Total DAC donors	4.98	6.76	8.79
Bilateral			
Australia	1.38	3.38	19.09
Austria	5.04	5.77	3.83
Belgium	1.73	0.00	6.42
Canada	9.17	8.01	5.31
Denmark	7.03	10.03	12.98
Finland	3.52	11.25	18.66
France	5.19	5.60	14.27
Germany	4.10	2.36	5.77
Italy	21.47	9.43	4.79
Japan	3.90	8.51	7.80
Netherlands	4.83	8.73	13.37
New Zealand	14.92	—	—
Norway	12.74	6.61	12.02
Portugal	—	0.00	0.45
Spain	—	3.03	7.55
Sweden	11.25	13.81	13.93
Switzerland	10.96	7.19	9.79
United Kingdom	0.65	9.32	9.78
United States	4.01	3.18	8.50
Multilateral			
African Development Fund	6.59	3.35	4.18
Asian Development Bank	5.37	8.96	6.86
Commission of the European Community	6.42	6.79	3.33
IDA	4.36	10.04	9.64
Inter-American Development Bank	6.56	1.62	1.97
International Fund for Agricultural Development	4.13	1.25	3.23

— Not available.
Source: CRS-DAC database.

The pattern of spending on IPGs and NPGs differs considerably by donor as follows:

- In 1980–82, of 17 bilateral donors 9 allocated more than the average (5 percent) of aid to IPGs, and 5 of these (in ascending order Switzerland, Sweden, Norway, New Zealand, and Italy) allocated more than 10 percent.

Table 5.2. Spending on National Public Goods as a Percentage of Aid, Selected Years, 1980–98

Donor	1980–82	1990–92	1996–98
Total DAC donors	11.24	21.67	29.40
Bilateral			
Australia	4.51	24.73	51.20
Austria	2.57	8.34	43.05
Belgium	0.62	2.90	27.18
Canada	19.85	11.27	26.85
Denmark	23.84	40.44	34.73
Finland	10.59	14.73	32.13
France	7.59	8.35	16.96
Germany	4.12	5.31	23.62
Italy	5.24	19.76	18.02
Japan	7.72	7.20	17.31
Netherlands	11.14	20.00	26.77
New Zealand	19.10	—	—
Norway	17.89	22.15	26.99
Portugal	—	1.25	0.93
Spain	—	5.11	30.09
Sweden	13.24	35.65	43.89
Switzerland	19.60	20.15	24.25
United Kingdom	1.95	28.36	27.97
United States	12.93	32.77	37.77
Multilateral			
African Development Fund	29.97	20.98	34.73
Asian Development Bank	6.33	25.53	47.34
Commission of the European Community	12.32	20.53	20.76
IDA	13.51	40.09	44.42
Inter-American Development Bank	21.57	38.19	69.15
International Fund for Agricultural Development	36.20	34.40	46.88

— Not available.
Source: CRS-DAC database.

- By 1990–92, 10 allocated more than 5 percent of aid to IPGs, and 4 allocated more than 10 percent (in ascending order Switzerland, Sweden, Denmark, and New Zealand).
- In 1996–98, only Austria and Portugal allocated less than 5 percent of aid to IPGs, and seven donors allocated more than 10 percent (in ascending order, Norway, Denmark, Netherlands, Sweden, France, Finland, and Australia).

Table 5.3. Spending on Public Goods as a Percentage of Aid, Selected Years, 1980–98

Donor	1980–82	1990–92	1996–98
Total DAC donors	16.22	28.43	38.19
Bilateral			
Australia	5.89	28.11	70.29
Austria	7.61	14.11	46.88
Belgium	2.35	2.90	33.60
Canada	29.02	19.28	32.16
Denmark	30.87	50.47	47.71
Finland	14.11	25.99	50.79
France	12.77	13.96	31.23
Germany	8.22	7.67	29.39
Italy	26.71	29.19	22.81
Japan	11.62	15.71	25.11
Netherlands	15.97	28.73	40.14
New Zealand	34.02	—	—
Norway	30.62	28.76	39.01
Portugal	—	1.25	1.38
Spain	—	8.14	37.65
Sweden	24.48	49.46	57.82
Switzerland	30.56	27.34	34.04
United Kingdom	2.61	37.68	37.75
United States	16.93	35.95	46.27
Multilateral			
African Development Fund	36.55	24.33	38.91
Asian Development Bank	11.70	34.49	54.20
Commission of the European Union	18.73	27.32	24.09
IDA	17.87	50.13	54.06
Inter-American Development Bank	28.13	39.81	71.12
International Fund for Agricultural Development	40.33	35.65	50.11

— Not available.

Note: Total public goods are the sum of NPGs and IPGs.

Source: CRS-DAC database.

- Of the multilateral donors covered, only IDA allocated as much as 10 percent of aid to IPGs in 1996–98, although the special operations fund of the IDB allocated 19 percent to IPGs in 1985–87 (not shown in the table).

- In general, the Nordic donors allocate a greater share of aid to IPGs than other donors do. Australia and Switzerland also feature well (data for New Zealand in the 1990s are not available).

- In 1980–82, nine bilateral donors allocated more than 10 percent of aid to NPGs (four allocated about 20 percent or more, namely, in ascending order, New Zealand, Switzerland, Canada, and Denmark), and five allocated less than 5 percent.

- In 1985–87, seven bilateral donors allocated more than 20 percent of aid to NPGs and five allocated less than 10 percent.

- In 1990–92, nine bilateral donors allocated about 20 percent or more to NPGs (Denmark, at 40 percent, and Sweden, at 36 percent, were the only ones above 30 percent), and seven allocated less than 10 percent.

- In 1996–98, seven bilaterals donors allocated more than 30 percent to NPGs (Australia, at 51 percent, being the highest), while only Portugal allocated less than 10 percent (it allocated almost nothing to NPGs).

- For the multilateral donors the pattern was more varied. The International Fund for Agricultural Development consistently allocated a third or more of aid to NPGs. The share of the Commission of the European Community has consistently been around 20 percent since the mid-1980s; IDA's share increased to more than 40 percent in the 1990s; the Asian Development Bank's share rose to more than 40 percent by the late 1990s; and the share of the African Development Fund has fluctuated, but was more than a third by the late 1990s.

- Although Nordic donors tended to allocate more aid to NPGs than other bilateral donors, the pattern was less pronounced than for IPGs. Southern European donors tended to allocate the least to both NPGs and IPGs. The multilateral donors tended to allocate a greater share of aid to NPGs than most bilateral donors.

Overall, the share of aid allocated to financing public goods has increased significantly. Of the 23 donors (bilateral and multilateral), 10 allocated 25 percent or more of aid to public goods in 1980–82, whereas by 1996–98 all but 3 allocated more than 20 percent and 9 allocated more than 40 percent. However, this implies that even by the late 1990s, more than half of aid was not spent on public goods.

The single most important item of aid expenditure that did not fall in the category of public goods was aid allocated to finance debt relief, especially in the 1990s. We do not classify debt relief and related spending as contributing to the provision of public goods, given the inherently high degree of excludability and rivalry in such expenditures. As discussed in chapter 2, such spending could be included as a complementary activity, and indeed, this is what World Bank (2001) does. Including such spending would increase the share of aid allocated to NPGs by about 10 percentage points in the 1990s, and is part of the reason why the World Bank (2001) estimates higher aid spending on public goods than we do. Arguably, discussions about the financing and delivery of debt relief should be kept separate from discussions about IPGs; there are moral and economic arguments for providing debt relief that do not depend on it providing a global public good.

Another major category of aid spending excluded here is financing, mostly of projects, for physical capital investment and for production activities. Although some investment provides a complementary activity that contributes to the national public good, for instance, roads, identifying this in the CRS data is not possible. In this sense we may underestimate spending on NPGs, although not on the more relevant IPGs.

We also exclude various other categories of aid spending, such as general balance of payments support, food aid, and financing for private sector development. Furthermore, we exclude any aid specifically allocated to poverty reduction, which is not identified in the CRS data. As argued in chapter 2, reducing poverty is a complementary activity that increases the public's ability to benefit from public goods. Within donor aid budgets, direct aid for poverty reduction has only assumed significance in recent years.

Figure 5.1 shows trends in the allocation of aid to public goods during 1980–98 broken down by NPGs and IPGs and by sector. The following patterns are apparent:

- The share of aid allocated to public goods has been rising and has roughly doubled since 1980.
- This rising trend is evident for NPGs and IPGs in all sectors except governance, which by definition is not an IPG.
- Environment attracted the greatest share, about half, of aid allocated to IPGs and NPGs, and its share increased in line with the share of aid allocated to public goods.
- Health and knowledge public goods attracted similar shares of aid, and both increased significantly in the 1990s (especially H-NPGs).

Figure 5.1. Aid Commitments by Bilateral and Multilateral Donors to National and International Public Goods, 1980–98

(percentage of aid)

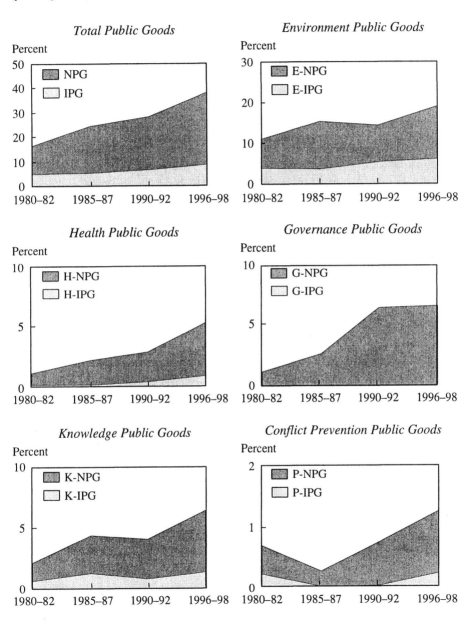

Source: CRS-DAC OECD database.

- The share of aid allocated to conflict prevention was small, although the shares of P-NPGs increased significantly since the mid-1980s and that of P-IPGs increased in the 1990s. Most spending on peacekeeping does not appear in aid budgets.
- Aid spending on G-NPGs rose in the late 1980s, but subsequently stabilized.

Aid Funding of Public Goods by Sector

Tables 5.4 to 5.6 summarize the proportion of IPG spending by sector. Note that by our strict definition, none of the spending on G appears, because it is classified as NPGs. The most striking pattern is that E-IPGs have consistently been the main sector, accounting for almost four-fifths of IPG spending in 1980–82 and 1990–92, although this fell to under 71 percent in 1996–98. The share of H more than doubled between 1980 and 1998, and in 1996–98 accounted for more than 11 percent. K stayed roughly steady at around 12 to 13 percent in 1980–82 and 1990–92, but rose to more than 15 percent in 1996–98. The share of P remained low, amounting to just over 2.5 percent in 1996–98. However, a less strict definition of P-IPGs that included aid to refugees would most certainly lead to a much higher share. Furthermore, significant spending on peacekeeping may not go through aid budgets.

The broad pattern for the allocation of total aid is also reflected among most donors with some exceptions. France, most notably, and Belgium to a lesser degree, both had a relatively high share of K in 1996–98, while Austria, Portugal, and Spain had an above average share of P. Certain donors—Belgium, the United Kingdom, and the United States—placed a much greater emphasis on health (H) than the average, with the share of each exceeding 20 percent. For 1996–98 the ranking of donors with respect to contributions to IPGs within sectors reveals the following:

- Japan, followed by IDA, the United States, and the Netherlands, allocated the highest shares to E-IPGs.
- IDA, followed by the United States, the United Kingdom, and Germany, allocated the most to H-IPGs.
- The United States, Sweden, and Spain allocated the highest shares to P-IPGs.
- France, IDA, and the Netherlands allocated the highest shares to K-IPGs.

Table 5.4. Aid Spending on IPGs, by Sector, as a Percentage of Total IPG Spending, 1980–82

Donor	E	H	P	K
Total DAC donors	78.30	4.10	4.20	13.40
Bilateral				
Australia	94.40	1.80	3.20	0.60
Austria	100.00	0.00	0.00	0.00
Belgium	100.00	0.00	0.00	0.00
Canada	82.00	0.60	0.20	17.20
Denmark	94.80	1.00	3.40	0.80
Finland	85.90	14.10	0.00	0.00
France	84.50	5.40	0.00	10.00
Germany	90.50	1.10	0.70	7.70
Italy	100.00	0.00	0.00	0.00
Japan	89.00	5.80	0.30	5.00
Netherlands	74.10	6.90	13.00	6.00
New Zealand	92.30	0.00	0.00	7.70
Norway	89.70	0.30	0.00	10.00
Portugal	—	—	—	—
Spain	—	—	—	—
Sweden	49.60	6.50	39.60	4.30
Switzerland	76.90	7.30	0.00	15.80
United Kingdom	97.50	0.00	0.00	2.50
United States	52.50	10.50	0.00	37.00
Multilateral				
African Development Fund	85.30	14.70	0.00	0.00
Asian Development Bank	100.00	0.00	0.00	0.00
Commission for the European Union	72.10	3.40	16.70	7.80
IDA	83.40	0.00	0.00	16.60
Inter-American Development Bank	100.00	0.00	0.00	0.00
International Fund for Agricultural Development	49.20	0.00	0.00	50.80

— Not available.
Source: CRS-DAC database.

These results on sectoral allocations are not surprising, and are largely driven by how IPGs are defined. The environment is a global commons, and environmental projects will tend to have identifiable spillovers. Even if these are not truly global, they are potentially transboundary, and hence international. Thus much of the spending on environmental projects and programs

Table 5.5. Aid Spending on IPGs, by Sector, as a Percentage of Total IPG Spending, 1990–92

Donor	E	H	P	K
Total DAC donors	80.70	6.80	0.20	12.30
Bilateral				
Australia	70.70	16.70	0.60	12.00
Austria	93.40	0.30	0.00	6.30
Belgium	—	—	—	—
Canada	82.50	8.20	0.00	9.20
Denmark	56.90	21.80	0.00	21.30
Finland	90.40	0.30	0.00	9.30
France	78.80	4.90	0.00	16.30
Germany	98.00	0.00	0.00	2.00
Italy	87.90	5.80	0.30	6.00
Japan	92.70	1.70	0.00	5.60
Netherlands	78.80	2.40	0.00	18.90
New Zealand	—	—	—	—
Norway	76.60	20.70	0.00	2.70
Portugal	—	—	—	—
Spain	93.30	0.00	0.00	6.70
Sweden	67.50	6.70	1.20	24.60
Switzerland	64.20	20.80	0.00	15.00
United Kingdom	61.40	8.00	0.00	30.60
United States	60.50	12.80	0.30	26.40
Multilateral				
African Development Fund	100.00	0.00	0.00	0.00
Asian Development Bank	100.00	0.00	0.00	0.00
Commission for the European Union	50.40	38.20	0.10	11.30
IDA	74.80	14.10	0.00	11.10
Inter-American Development Bank	83.70	0.00	0.00	16.30
International Fund for Agricultural Development	100.00	0.00	0.00	0.00

— Not available.
Source: CRS-DAC database.

can be classified as spending on IPGs. This is not so readily true of spending on health and education, much of which is more in the nature of NPGs than IPGs. Spending on such goods is a greater share of NPG spending than of IPG spending. The most extreme example is of governance, as we classify all spending on G as spending on NPGs. Furthermore, considerable spending on

Table 5.6. Aid Spending on IPGs, by Sector, as a Percentage of Total IPG Spending, 1996–98

Donor	E	H	P	K
Total DAC donors	70.50	11.40	2.60	15.50
Bilateral				
Australia	87.60	6.40	2.10	3.90
Austria	41.40	2.60	40.30	15.70
Belgium	29.90	32.00	10.60	27.50
Canada	72.90	12.20	7.70	7.10
Denmark	93.70	3.30	2.40	0.60
Finland	87.60	1.00	4.60	6.80
France	23.80	2.00	0.00	74.20
Germany	80.20	16.90	0.00	2.90
Italy	80.30	11.60	2.70	5.50
Japan	96.90	1.70	0.00	1.40
Netherlands	72.20	10.10	2.00	15.60
New Zealand	—	—	—	—
Norway	59.00	9.40	6.00	25.60
Portugal	22.10	0.00	73.50	4.30
Spain	49.60	5.30	17.70	27.50
Sweden	62.30	7.80	7.40	22.50
Switzerland	72.90	13.90	0.50	12.70
United Kingdom	56.10	29.40	3.30	11.20
United States	61.80	21.90	7.30	9.10
Multilateral				
African Development Fund	100.00	0.00	0.00	0.00
Asian Development Bank	100.00	0.00	0.00	0.00
Commission for the European Union	53.90	25.00	5.80	15.30
IDA	59.20	23.20	1.10	16.50
Inter-American Development Bank	100.00	0.00	0.00	0.00
International Fund for Agricultural Development	100.00	0.00	0.00	0.00

— Not available.
Source: CRS-DAC database.

some IPGs may be missed from this approach. Peacekeeping and relevant research, for example, may not be financed out of aid budgets.

Table 5.7 presents a similar breakdown of aid spending on NPGs by sector for 1980–82 and 1996–98. The distribution of NPG spending over sectors is similar to that of IPG spending, with the following differences:

Table 5.7. Aid Spending on NPGs, by Sector, as a Percentage of Total NPG Spending, 1980–82 and 1996–98

	1980–82					1996–98				
Donor	E	H	G	P	K	E	H	G	P	K
Total DAC donors	63.82	8.68	9.92	4.20	13.37	43.27	14.44	21.85	3.43	17.01
Bilateral										
Australia	73.96	0.02	5.70	6.39	13.93	6.21	11.26	43.40	1.14	37.99
Austria	0.43	0.00	99.57	0.00	0.00	28.81	12.26	4.55	3.20	51.17
Belgium	100.00	0.00	0.00	0.00	0.00	33.25	22.98	14.45	4.10	25.22
Canada	69.40	2.18	12.67	5.35	10.40	30.08	6.91	39.02	6.72	17.27
Denmark	81.37	9.13	0.32	0.00	9.17	37.48	27.02	12.76	7.92	14.82
Finland	3.49	56.34	40.18	0.00	0.00	31.62	17.01	24.71	8.45	18.20
France	31.63	10.98	44.59	2.79	10.01	54.04	7.64	22.29	1.01	15.01
Germany	69.43	6.51	7.95	8.72	7.38	74.60	5.08	3.52	0.38	16.41
Italy	78.90	9.09	0.00	0.00	12.00	33.43	14.40	12.15	2.15	37.87
Japan	76.01	16.43	3.53	0.00	4.02	68.09	6.62	13.54	0.00	11.75
Netherlands	53.31	21.43	17.69	2.19	5.37	28.28	17.78	17.89	15.79	20.26
New Zealand	72.26	1.30	17.12	2.42	6.90	—	—	—	—	—
Norway	21.86	34.31	26.95	4.42	12.47	32.57	12.17	23.95	10.12	21.19
Portugal	—	—	—	—	—	0.00	48.81	14.36	0.00	36.83
Spain	—	—	—	—	—	19.70	37.17	13.40	3.23	26.49
Sweden	51.94	12.48	6.95	15.03	13.60	24.95	12.65	29.70	15.37	17.33
Switzerland	30.26	10.36	9.25	1.54	48.58	35.51	15.01	26.89	5.16	17.43
United Kingdom	5.84	0.24	16.03	69.40	8.49	25.49	13.62	21.16	1.53	38.19
United States	59.95	7.66	14.50	5.42	12.47	37.87	15.13	37.30	2.64	7.07
Multilateral										
African Development Fund	76.96	16.27	0.00	0.00	6.77	34.51	9.93	23.82	11.76	19.97
Asian Development Bank	28.75	18.75	3.12	12.50	36.87	62.52	5.76	8.22	0.00	23.50
Commission for the European Union	76.02	3.50	4.72	0.82	14.94	24.63	18.43	28.08	17.38	11.47
IDA	61.40	6.61	7.76	0.52	23.71	36.37	25.50	19.27	0.80	18.05
Inter-American Development Bank	65.15	5.66	2.79	9.11	17.28	64.83	0.00	32.63	0.00	2.54
International Fund for Agricultural Development	92.19	0.00	0.00	7.81	0.00	100.00	0.00	0.00	0.00	0.00

— Not available.
Source: CRS-DAC database.

- A relatively large and growing share of NPG spending was allocated to G.
- In 1996–98 Australia, Canada, and the United States spent more than a third of their shares on G-IPGs.
- By the late 1980s (not shown in the table) the share of aid spending on H-NPG and K-NPG was larger than on H-IPG and K-IPG, while the share of E-NPG was smaller than that of E-IPG.
- In 1996–98 IDA, Denmark, Portugal, and Spain spent more than a quarter of their NPG spending on H.
- In 1996–98 the Commission of the European Community, the Netherlands, and Sweden spent more than 10 percent of their shares on P-NPGs.

Spending on Public Goods in Developing Countries as a Share of Donor GDP

Donors that allocate more aid to IPGs do not necessarily spend more on IPGs in real terms; the real value (or cost to the donor) depends on the ODA to GDP ratio. However, donors that have a high IPG to ODA ratio apparently tend to allocate a higher share of GDP to the financing of IPGs. This section summarizes some of the main findings in relation to spending on public goods through the aid budget as a share of donor GDP (tables 5.8 to 5.10).

- With the exception of Sweden during 1990–92, donors committed less than 1/10th of 1 percent of GDP to IPGs over 1980–98.
- On average, donors committed 0.013 percent of GDP to IPGs in 1980–92, 0.017 percent in 1985–87 (figures for 1985–87 are available on request), 0.022 percent over 1990–92, and 0.027 percent in 1996–98.
- The same average percentages for NPGs are 0.022 percent in 1980–82, 0.046 percent in 1985–87, 0.055 percent in 1990–92, and 0.073 percent in 1996–98.
- This implies that for every US$1,000 generated in donor countries, an average of US$1 goes to aid financing of public goods, with 27 cents allocated to IPGs and 73 cents to NPGs.
- Variation across countries is considerable. The northern Europeans generally have a higher share of IPGs to GDP. By 1998 the Netherlands led the donors with less than 1/10th of 1 percent of GDP allocated to IPGs,

Table 5.8. Spending on Public Goods as a Percentage of Donors' GDP, Selected Years, 1980–98

Donor	1980–82	1990–92	1996–98
Australia	0.014	0.038	0.184
Austria	0.021	0.022	0.078
Belgium	0.003	0.003	0.069
Canada	0.047	0.041	0.063
Denmark	0.108	0.171	0.239
Finland	0.008	0.111	0.087
France	0.025	0.032	0.059
Germany	0.028	0.026	0.045
Italy	0.011	0.053	0.013
Japan	0.033	0.045	0.071
Netherlands	0.064	0.115	0.219
Norway	0.081	0.115	0.191
Portugal	0	0.001	0.001
Spain	0	0.013	0.049
Sweden	0.115	0.434	0.269
Switzland	0.045	0.069	0.067
United Kingdom	0.004	0.057	0.055
United States	0.025	0.048	0.031

Source: CRS-DAC database.

while Germany, Italy, and the United States brought up the rear, with less than 1/100th of 1 percent of GDP allocated to IPGs via aid.

- Sweden consistently led the group of donors with respect to the sum of IPG and NPG lending as a ratio of GDP, closely followed by the other northern European countries.
- By 1998, 13 donors still spent less than 1/10th of 1 percent of GDP on aid-financed public goods, 5 donors spent between 1/10th and 2/10ths (Norway and Australia), and 3 donors spent more than 2/10ths of 1 percent (Sweden, Denmark, and the Netherlands).

Because the share of aid allocated to IPGs almost doubled during the years under review, the share of GDP going to IPGs also doubled, albeit from a relatively low level. One implication of this is that the aid to GDP ratio, on average,

Table 5.9. Spending on IPGs as a Percentage of Donors' GDP, Selected Years, 1980–98

Donor	1980–82	1990–92	1996–98
Australia	0.003	0.005	0.050
Austria	0.014	0.009	0.006
Belgium	0.002	0	0.013
Canada	0.015	0.017	0.010
Denmark	0.025	0.034	0.065
Finland	0.002	0.048	0.032
France	0.010	0.013	0.027
Germany	0.014	0.008	0.009
Italy	0.009	0.017	0.003
Japan	0.011	0.024	0.022
Netherlands	0.019	0.035	0.073
Norway	0.034	0.026	0.059
Portugal	—	0	0
Spain	—	0.005	0.010
Sweden	0.053	0.121	0.065
Switzland	0.016	0.018	0.019
United Kingdom	0.001	0.014	0.014
United States	0.006	0.004	0.006

— Not available.
Source: CRS-DAC database.

changed little. An implication is that aid allocated to IPGs displaced aid allocated to other activities.

Three points are worth emphasizing regarding the results reported here. First, this chapter focuses on the financing of IPG provision in developing countries. Rich countries may allocate significant amounts to IPG provision, especially research, within their own countries or regionally, for example, the European Union. This chapter does not address such spending. Second, many IPGs are inherently inter-related and their classification in a particular sector may be arbitrary. For example, agricultural research contributes to global knowledge, but also contributes to environmental policy and interventions. Third, the provision of NPGs may be essential to facilitate the provision of IPGs by developing countries, reflecting the issue of complementary activities.

Table 5.10. Spending on NPGs as a Percentage of Donors' GDP, Selected Years, 1980–98

Donor	1980–82	1990–92	1996–98
Australia	0.011	0.033	0.134
Austria	0.007	0.013	0.072
Belgium	0.001	0.003	0.056
Canada	0.032	0.024	0.053
Denmark	0.083	0.137	0.174
Finland	0.006	0.063	0.055
France	0.015	0.019	0.032
Germany	0.014	0.018	0.036
Italy	0.002	0.036	0.010
Japan	0.022	0.021	0.049
Netherlands	0.045	0.080	0.146
Norway	0.047	0.089	0.132
Portugal	—	0.001	0.001
Spain	—	0.008	0.039
Sweden	0.062	0.313	0.204
Switzland	0.029	0.051	0.048
United Kingdom	0.003	0.043	0.041
United States	0.019	0.044	0.025

— Not available.
Source: CRS-DAC database.

DOES AID FOR IPGS DISPLACE OTHER AID?

This section uses simple regressions for an exploratory analysis of the CRS data to shed light on whether aid (ODA) spending on IPGs is additional to traditional ODA spending, or whether it merely substitutes for other forms of aid. If aid spending on IPGs is additional, we can be more confident that aid offers a potential source of increased net funding for providing public goods in developing countries. The argument is that increased funds for IPGs are required to deal with the emergence of new global "bads," such as environmental problems, which may affect global problems directly, and hence there may be a self-interest for more spending on IPGs (see Kaul, Grunberg, and Stern 1999; World Bank 2001).

One of the channels through which countries can spend more on IPGs is through aid. Countries can decide to spend more on IPGs as well as on aid generally. However, spending on IPGs may simply displace aid for other purposes. Donors can have a genuine rationale for this if spending on IPGs, for instance, through a network approach, is more efficient and effective than traditional ODA in reducing poverty. However, more generally, donors may decide to spend more on IPGs for various reasons, and while they may regard ODA spending as one of the main channels, they may also keep total ODA spending in check. Donors may feel that financing public goods is a better use of aid.[3] In such situations, donors replace traditional non-IPG aid with IPG aid. Countries can thus decide to spend more on IPGs but not increase aid in proportion. The evidence presented in the previous section that spending on IPGs increased as a share of aid, and hence increased faster than aid increased, suggests that this has indeed been the case.

Regression analysis reinforces the conclusion that spending on public goods has taken away from other forms of aid-financed expenditures. We first examine whether changes over time in the share of IPGs in ODA are related to changes in the share of ODA in donor countries' GDP. We find little correlation between these two variables: while the share of IPGs has increased, aid to GDP has either remained stable or has fallen. We also find that donors with a larger share of IPGs in their aid budget are likely to be more generous donors, but that this effect has weakened over time. Thus, even the less generous donors have stepped up their funding of IPGs. Putting the two findings together, we conclude that over time, the rise in the share of IPGs has essentially come at the expense of other forms of aid.

We begin by estimating a simple regression of the form

$$\Delta ODASH_{it} = \beta \Delta IPGSH_{it} + \gamma + \gamma_1 TD_{85-87} + \gamma_2 TD_{90-92} \qquad (5.1)$$

where Δ is the first difference operator; $ODASH_{it}$ is the share of ODA in total GDP (current value) for country i at time t; $IPGSH_{it}$ is the share of ODA spending on IPGs; TD is a time dummy; and α, β, and the γs are parameters to estimate. If spending on IPGs is additional to traditional ODA, we should find that a rise in the proportion of ODA spent on IPGs is associated with a rise in the ratio of ODA to donor GDP, other things being equal, and hence β is greater than 0. By taking first differences, we sweep out the country-specific effects and, hence, consider within country changes, that is, the change between periods in a particular donor's IPG to ODA ratio related to the change in that donor's ODA to GDP ratio during the same time period. We use the CRS-DAC data discussed previously, and donor observations are for the four different three-year averages: 1980–82, 1985–87, 1990–92, and 1996–98. The analysis is based on 16 bilateral donors: Australia, Austria, Belgium, Canada, Denmark, Finland, France, Germany, Italy, Japan, the Netherlands, Norway, Sweden, Switzerland, the United Kingdom, and the United States.

The results are presented in table 5.11. These show a small secular increase in the ODA to GDP ratio in 1985–87 and 1990–92 and a decline thereafter, although the coefficients are not significant at the conventional levels. For our purpose, the finding is that an increase in the share of aid allocated to IPGs is not associated with a rise in the ODA to GDP ratio.

Table 5.11. Does IPG Spending Lead to More ODA Spending over Time?

$$\Delta ODASH_{it} = \beta \Delta IPGSH_{it} + \gamma + \gamma_1 TD_{85-87} + \gamma_2 TD_{90-92} \qquad (5.1)$$

Parameter	Coefficient estimate	t-statistics
β	0.0036	0.85
γ	–0.0005	–1.29
γ_1	0.0008	1.52
γ_2	0.0008	1.69
Rbar-squared (adjusted)	0.07	
Observations	48	

Note: Pooled ordinary least squares estimates.
Source: Authors' calculations.

A slightly different approach is to reverse equation (5.1) to test whether an increasing ODA to GDP ratio is associated with an increasing IPG to ODA ratio over time as follows:

$$\Delta IPGSH_{it} = \beta \Delta ODASH_{it} + \gamma + \gamma_1 TD_{85-87} + \gamma_2 TD_{90-92} \qquad (5.1a)$$

The results are presented in table 5.12. Again we find β to be insignificant. We do find evidence for a notable increase in the IPG share of ODA toward the end of the period, that is, during 1996–98, compared with 1990–92 ($\gamma > 0$), but this is not related to the ODA to GDP ratio.[4] These results suggest that spending on IPGs is displacing other forms of aid.

Table 5.12. Does the ODA to GDP Ratio Influence the IPG to ODA Ratio over Time?

$$\Delta IPGSH_{it} = \beta \Delta ODASH_{it} + \gamma + \gamma_1 TD_{85-87} + \gamma_2 TD_{90-92} \qquad (5.1a)$$

Parameter	Coefficient estimate	t-statistics
β	4.52	0.85
γ	0.035	2.92*
γ_1	−0.048	−2.82*
γ_2	−0.021	−1.22
Rbar-squared (adjusted)	0.16	
Observations	48	

* Significant at the 5 percent level.
Note: Pooled ordinary least squares estimates.
Source: Authors' calculations.

We can also look at country variations to see, in effect, if the ranking of donors by the IPG to ODA ratio is related to the ranking of donors according to the ODA to GDP ratio:

$$ODASH_i = \alpha + \beta IPGSH_i. \qquad (5.2)$$

We perform this regression for each period for which we have observations, and hence do not index by time. The results are presented in table 5.13. We find that a significant proportion (up to 50 percent) in the variation of ODA as a percentage of GDP can be explained by the share of ODA spent on IPGs in some time periods (β is significant in three of the four periods). Thus donors that allocate more aid to IPGs also tend to allocate more of their GDP to aid. Naturally, given that this is a cross-sectional correlation, similar patterns exist if we reverse equation (5.2).[5]

The implication of these results is that there is a significant correlation between ODA to GDP and IPG to ODA ratios across countries, but that this relationship had diminished by the late 1990s. Given the absence of a relationship between the ratios over time, the implication is that, especially in the late 1990s, most donors increased the amount of aid allocated to IPGs, but without an associated increase in their aid to GDP ratio. Thus spending on IPGs tends to displace other aid spending.

Table 5.13. The Cross-Country Relationship, Selected Years, 1980–82 to 1996–98

$$ODASH_i = \alpha + \beta IPGSH_i \qquad (5\text{-}2)$$

Parameter	1980–82		1985–87		1990–92		1996–98	
α	0.0023	(4.46)*	0.0010	(2.07)*	0.0005	(0.56)	0.001	(1.20)
β	−0.0016	(−0.26)	0.027	(3.75)*	0.034	(3.23)*	0.014	(1.76)**
R-squared (adjusted)	0.01		0.50		0.43		0.24	
Observations	16		16		16		16	

* Significant at the 5 percent level.
** Significant at the 10 percent level.
Note: t-statistics are in parentheses.
Source: Authors' calculations.

This would be cause for concern if the areas of aid spending that were reduced were NPGs; however, as shown earlier, this does not appear to be the case. Increased aid spending on public goods has probably replaced spending previously allocated to investment projects, many of which will essentially have been private goods in nature. Arguably, such investment would be more productive if financed privately, and funding public goods may be a better use of aid. Nevertheless, the situation needs to be monitored. If spending on IPGs were to displace aid spending on complementary NPGs, the effect would weaken developing countries' ability to provide IPGs.

CASE STUDIES OF BILATERAL DONORS: THE UNITED KINGDOM AND THE NETHERLANDS

The analysis thus far has allowed us to estimate the allocation of aid to IPGs for a variety of donors using a standard dataset. This section investigates in more detail the types of IPGs financed by examining individual donor aid statistics. The principal aim is to illustrate that CRS data tend to underestimate aid spending on IPGs. Note that the figures used are based on disbursements or budget expenditure plans, rather than on commitments data underlying the CRS, and there may not be a close correspondence between the two sets of figures. In the case of the Netherlands we also try to identify some expenditures on IPGs that are not financed out of the aid budget, but such data are incomplete. In addition, donor practices differ and no countries collate all spending on IPGs. Support for the Global Environment Facility provides an example: all donors allocate some aid to this, but some donors also allocate funds from the budget of the ministry for the environment or an equivalent agency.

The United Kingdom

Like other donors, the United Kingdom does not classify aid disbursements according to criteria that are clearly related to public goods. Specifically, *British Aid Statistics* does not provide a breakdown of bilateral aid programs by sectoral allocation. Adopting our earlier classifications is not a major problem, as most such aid is for NPGs. However, some of the categories defined in the statistics can be allocated to IPGs. This is done using statistics on aid disbursements, and the results are reported in table 5.14 for fiscal years 1996/97–1998/99.

In table 5.14 various bilateral programs are allocated to one of four IPG sectors. Humanitarian (P-IPGs) comprised expenditure by the Conflict and Humanitarian Affairs Department. This was mostly on emergency response (but excluded in-country spending for ongoing emergencies, which was included, but not separately identified in, country programs) and conflict and humanitarian policy, but also included a small amount of food aid in fiscal 1996/97. Education (K-IPG) was expenditure by the Education Division and was mostly Commonwealth and Chevening Scholarships (included as capacity building), but also had funds for research and university links. Knowledge was spending by the Environmental Policy Department and the Rural Livelihoods Department on renewable natural resources research (hence classed as K). Health (H) was spending by the Health and Population Division, mostly on health and population and reproductive health access (plans for 2000 and later include significant amounts for malaria, HIV/AIDS, and poliomyelitis).

Other expenditures on IPGs were from the Multilateral Programme (and corresponded to the same Department for International Development departments or divisions listed above). Humanitarian (P) consisted mostly of the World Food Program and multilateral partnerships. Knowledge included small amounts for desertification research in fiscal 1998/99, but was mostly international

Table 5.14. British Aid Allocated to IPGs, Fiscal Years 1996/97–1998/99

Destination of aid	1996/97	1997/98	1998/99
Total (£ millions)	2,019.60	1,979.30	2,238.60
Bilateral (percentage of total aid)	52.62	51.68	50.14
Humanitarian (P)	4.43	2.90	0.93
Education (E)	1.43	1.46	1.26
Knowledge (K)	1.52	1.41	1.46
Health (H)	1.07	1.12	0.93
Multilateral (percentage of total aid)	47.36	48.34	49.84
Humanitarian (P)	0.38	1.31	1.76
Knowledge (K)	0.38	0.32	0.34
Health (H)	1.42	1.34	1.04
International Fund for Agricultural Development (E)	0.09	0.14	0.09
Food and Agriculture Organization of the United Nations	0.53	0.56	0.45
United Nations Children's Fund (H)	0.45	0.40	0.45
United Nations Development Programme	1.39	1.12	1.34
United Nations Educational, Scientific, and Cultural Organization (K)	0.00	0.80	0.50
United Nations Relief and Works Agency funding from the Western Asia Department (P)	0.40	0.51	0.15
IPGs by sector (percentage of total aid)			
K	3.33	3.99	3.56
H	2.94	2.86	2.42
E	0.62	0.70	0.54
P	5.21	4.72	2.84
Total	12.10	12.27	9.36

Source: Department for International Development (2000, annex 1).

renewable natural resources research (hence classed as K). Health was mostly the United Nations Fund for Population and international health, including the World Health Organization. The United Nations AIDS Programme is included in plans after 2000. We also list expenditure from the United Nations and Commonwealth Department on the International Fund for Agricultural Development and the Food and Agricultural Organization of the United Nations (classed as E); on the United Nations Educational, Scientific, and Cultural Organization (classed as K); the United Nations Children's Fund (classed as H); and the United Nations Development Programme (not classed as an IPG). The final entry is the United Nations Relief and Works Agency funding from the Western Asia Department (classed as P).

Given the way the statistics are reported, this approach provides incomplete coverage of expenditure on IPGs out of British aid. We will shortly discuss some expenditures that may be missed here (mostly directed through the World Bank). On the basis of these figures, about 12 percent of British aid is allocated to IPGs (on a strict definition). Although the share was lower than 12 percent in fiscal 1998/99, plans for fiscal 1999/00 and thereafter suggest that this is atypical, and the 12 percent share may increase. This percentage corresponds to a volume expenditure of about £240 million per year in the late 1990s, and is somewhat higher that the 10 percent estimated from CRS data.

Another way to identify British spending on IPGs is to examine its financing of trust fund programs and activities (TFPA) operated through the World Bank. Most trust fund money finances IPGs, although it includes funding for highly indebted poor country debt relief, which we do not classify as an IPG. Also included are emergency funds intended for specific countries or regions, but these can be treated as IPGs. During 1996–2000 the United Kingdom contributed, on average, some US$80 million per year to the TFPA, rising from US$50 million in 1996 to US$121 million in 2000 (but almost half of this related to heavily indebted poor countries). Clearly this is only a proportion of British financing of IPGs, and much double-counting between this and the estimates in table 5.14 is unlikely.

Some categories included in TFPA are not IPGs, such as debt relief, consultants' funds, and International Finance Corporation activities. Deducting these, the United Kingdom allocated some US$244 million to IPGs through the TFPA during 1996–2000. The largest single component of this was financing for the Global Environment Facility (36 percent), and a further 20 percent went toward other co-financing schemes. The second largest single item was also environmental, with 7 percent going to the Ozone Phase-Out Trust Fund under the Montreal Protocol. Other individual allocations accounted for less than 3 percent of the total, and many were extremely small amounts. Combining the funds allocated to TFPA with the estimates in table 5.14 suggests a total of no more than £300 million per year of British aid being spent on IPGs in the late 1990s. This would correspond to about 15 percent of British aid being allocated to IPGs, considerably higher than the estimate of 10 percent in 1996–98 using CRS data. As the CRS data omit some items we have been able to identify here, and the share has been rising, 15 percent is a reasonable figure for 2000.

The Netherlands

The IPG concept is relatively new to the Netherlands, and no official policy statements on this issue are available. We therefore limit the discussion to an analysis of what the Dutch spend on IPGs by classifying all expenditure relevant to foreign policy. Even such a classification is not straightforward, as the Dutch budget does not distinguish between IPGs and non-IPGs, thus our results are inevitably somewhat subjective.

Based on CRS data, we estimate that by the late 1990s some 13 percent of Dutch aid could be classified as spending on IPGs. However, there is other spending on IPGs under separate budgets of individual departments, not only foreign affairs or development cooperation, but also other departments such as education or defense. We initially focus on classifying all expenditure related to international cooperation. While more inclusive than the ODA budget, it excludes spending in the Netherlands, for example, on health research.

The Dutch budget includes the so-called homogenous group international cooperation (HGIS) budget, which brings together all expenditure related to international cooperation. The HGIS budget includes expenditure on ODA and also on items such as the environment, under the Joint Implementation and Clean Development Mechanisms, and on peacekeeping operations that fall under the Department of Defense. Total expenditure on international cooperation was planned to be 1.1 percent of GNP in 2000, of which 0.8 percent was classified as ODA. Table 5.15 breaks down actual integrated spending on international cooperation in 1999.

Table 5.15. HGIS Spending, 1999

(NLG thousands)

Spending on	Integrated budget	Of which ODA
Governance	136,596	33,595
Conflict prevention	1,258,045	691,946
European integration	23,318	0
Sustainable poverty alleviation	6,370,396	5,584,100
Bilateral agreements	1,224,079	293,473
Other	1,122,786	306,683
Total	10,135,220	6,909,797
As a percentage of GNP	1.1	0.8

Source: Ministry of Foreign Affairs (2000).

If we look at the differences between ODA and overall HGIS spending on the six categories in table 5.15, we obtain insight into whether there is additional non-ODA spending on IPGs. The differences between ODA and overall HGIS spending are mainly due to statutory UN contributions in the category governance. There is a considerable difference between ODA and HGIS overall spending on conflict prevention, which is related to peacekeeping operations falling under the budget of the Department of Defense worth NLG 456 million. This is not counted as ODA, but could be thought of as spending on an IPG (conflict prevention). The difference in the category sustainable poverty alleviation is due to subsidies on loans by the Dutch Investment Bank, royal expenditure, contributions to the European Union budget, and grants to the FMO (Nederlandse Financieringsmaatschappij voor Ontwikkelingslanden NV, a semigovernmental development bank), all of which can hardly be counted as spending on IPGs. However, there is also the subcategory international educational research, of which NLG 6 million has been classified as non-ODA, but could be thought of as IPG spending (knowledge). However, most differences between ODA and overall HGIS spending in the categories bilateral agreements (for example, promotion of Dutch economic relations) and other (for instance, personnel costs of the Ministry of Foreign Affairs) are not IPG related. We conclude that a considerable amount of non-ODA money in the HGIS budget can be classified as spending on IPGs.

Obtaining a detailed picture of total spending on IPGs in the Netherlands is difficult, simply because the Dutch budget does not distinguish between IPGs and non-IPGs. We thus have to rely on our own judgments on what is an IPG and what is not. We use the HGIS budget for 1999, which provides an itemized list for HGIS (ODA and non-ODA) disbursements. Table 5.16 lists items from the HGIS budget that may be classified as IPGs. For each item we distinguish between ODA and non-ODA spending. The main category, which does fall under IPGs but not under ODA spending, is peacekeeping operations worth NLG 456 million.

We find that 27 percent of ODA is IPG related, and 25 percent of all HGIS spending is IPG related. If we take out the contributions to multilateral organizations, we arrive at 13 and 12 percent, respectively. The former figure is identical to that obtained from CRS data (which excludes aid delivered through multilateral agencies), but the non-aid HGIS spending on IPGs suggests that the Netherlands spends at least twice as much on IPGs in developing countries as the CRS estimates suggest. There are a number of important caveats. First,

Table 5.16. Actual Performance, HGIS Spending, 1999

(NLG thousands)

Description	Total	ODA	IPG
European Development Fund (part for environment)	8,847	8,847	IO
Security policy, etc.	92,671	60,852	P
Environmental policy in developing countries	308,152	300,570	E
Environmental education	2,000	2,000	E
Programma Voedselzekerheid en Voedingsverbetering Food Security Programme	30,000	30,000	IO/H
United Nations Fund for Population Activities, United Nations AIDS Programme, United Nations Children's Fund	155,500	155,500	IO
International education (spending by Ministry of Foreign Affairs)	265,372	231,877	K
Maatschappelijke Transformatie in Midden-en Oost Europe (part for environment)	13,000	0	E
United Nations Development Programme	155,000	155,000	IO
World Bank partnership	93,693	93,693	K/E
Other IO contributions	98,787	22,911	IO
International Fund for Agricultural Development, United Nations Capital Development Fund, World Food Program	84,984	84,984	IO
Yugoslavia, prisons	10,000	10,000	P
International education (spending by Ministry of Education) and research	96,052	94,622	K
Multilateral banks	611,881	611,881	IO
Peacekeeping operations	456,358	0	P
International environmental policy	12,431	840	E
International Civil Navigation Organization, International Maritime Organization, Universal Post Union/International Trade Union, World Meteorological Organization	1,547	53	IO
International technology	3,843	0	K
International organizations	13,578	0	IO
Other Food and Agriculture Organization of the United Nations	10,339	5,459	IO
Other United Nations Environment Programme	535	535	IO
Total IPG	2,524,570	1,869,624	
Total IPG, minus IO	1,353,572	794,454	
Total HGIS spending	10,135,220	6,909,797	
IPGs to HGIS ratio (total)	0.249	0.271	
IPGs to HGIS ratio (less spending by IO)	0.134	0.115	

IO International organizations (global governance institutions); other abbreviations in the IPG column as defined earlier.

Source: Ministry of Foreign Affairs (2000).

some categories such as international education may only partly be directed at IPGs, while the rest is for NPGs. This would lower the percentages given above. Second, we may not have included sufficient spending, for instance, by not taking into account IPG-related spending on bilateral programs. Third, we have not accounted for IPG spending that is not related to international cooperation in terms of the budget. For instance, spending on research on understanding communicable diseases conducted in the Netherlands will generally not be included in the HGIS budget. As with any exercise of this type, the estimates are no more than indicative.

Implications of Case Studies for CRS-Based Estimates of IPG Spending

We limited our case studies to two bilateral donors, largely because the detailed data required to identify total spending on IPGs is difficult to obtain. Clearly the estimates of aid allocation to IPGs using CRS commitment data (the only internationally comparable dataset) understate actual spending on IPGs outside donor countries. We can reasonably posit that the CRS data underestimate the volume of donor spending on IPGs in developing countries by about 50 percent. For the United Kingdom, we estimate that in 2000 some 15 percent of aid was allocated to IPGs, compared with some 10 percent using the CRS data. Similarly, the estimates suggest that the Netherlands may have spent more than 20 percent of aid on IPGs, whereas the CRS estimate was about 13 percent. Of course, this would not apply for all donors, but would be a useful benchmark figure on aggregate.

CONCLUSIONS

The share of aid allocated to IPGs has risen since the early 1980s. This has been confirmed by previous studies (Raffer 1998; World Bank 2001) and is not a disputed finding. This chapter examined the share of aid allocated to international and national public goods in total and by individual donors. We estimate that in the late 1990s donors allocated almost 10 percent of aid to IPGs and nearly 30 percent to NPGs. This is much more conservative than Raffer (1998), who includes as IPGs items we refer to as NPGs. It is, however, a bigger estimate than the share the World Bank (2001) allocated to core (international) public goods—4 percent in the late 1990s—as that study allocated items we have treated as IPGs to complementary public goods (more than 15 percent). The estimates here are based on CRS-DAC commitment data. We provided some evidence that the use of CRS data may lead to an underestimation of the share of aid allocated to IPGs by some 50 percent. Thus our estimates suggest that in the late 1990s, 15 to 20 percent of aid by bilateral donors was allocated to providing IPGs in developing countries.

The empirical analysis also showed that the share of aid allocated to financing public goods has doubled in the past two decades, and this has been broadly true for both IPGs and NPGs. Aid allocated to environmental public goods has remained at more than half of this total. In the 1990s in particular, increasing shares of aid were allocated to health, knowledge, and conflict prevention, all of which are core activities providing IPGs. As perceptions of the need to finance the provision of IPGs in developing countries have increased, so too has the share of aid allocated to public goods. As there are complementarities between national and international public goods (and many aspects of the IPG and NPG distinction are imprecise), it is appropriate that funding on each is increasing in unison.

This begs the question of whether aid can support increases in spending on IPGs in the future. In the past two decades, increased aid spending on public goods has been at the expense of other types of aid spending. Some of these other types of spending may be desirable in their own right, for example, schemes targeted directly at poverty reduction, or may generate externalities and benefits that contribute to growth and development, for instance, capital infrastructure projects. The real value of aid spending in these areas should not be reduced. Furthermore, debt relief can be justified on moral and economic grounds, but when granted, it would appear as an increase in aid (given donors' accounting methods), and hence may also substitute for other types of aid. The implication is that future increases in spending on IPGs in developing countries should not come from further increasing the share of aid allocated to this purpose. Consequently, either the value of aid should be increased or sources of funding other than aid are required to increase support for IPGs.

APPENDIX 5A. CRS CATEGORIES CLASSIFIED AS INTERNATIONAL AND NATIONAL PUBLIC GOODS

Sector	IPGs	NPGs
H	Infectious disease control (12250) Sexually transmitted disease control; HIV/AIDS (13040)	Health sector (12xxx) Family Planning (13030) Population policy (13010) Reproductive health care (13020) Population/reproductive health (13081) Water supply (14020) Sanitation (14030) Education and training in water supply and sanitation (14081) Social Services (16310)
E	River development (14040) Waste management (14050) Energy education (23081) Energy research (23082) Forestry policy (31210) Forestry development (31220) Fishery policy (31310) Fishery development (31320) Environmental policy (41010) Biosphere protection (41020) Biodiversity (41030) Site preservation (41040) Flood prevention (41050) Environmental education and training (41081) Environmental research (41082) Water resources policy (14010) Water resources protection (14015)	Low-cost housing (16220) Housing policy (16210) Solar energy (23067) Wind power (23068) Ocean power (23069) Biomass (23070) Energy pollution and management (23010) Geothermal energy (23066) Agriculture policy and administrative management (31110) Agricultural development (31120) Agricultural land resources (31130) Agrarian reform (31164) Agriculture alternative development (31165)
G		Policy and planning (15010) Public sector management (15020) Legal and judicial (15030) Government administration (15040) Civil society (15050) Employment policy and administrative management (16110) General government services (16320) Financial policy (24010) Monetary institutions (24020) Trade policy (33110)

(Appendix continues on the following page.)

APPENDIX 5A. (CONTINUED)

Sector	IPGs	NPGs
P	Peace building (15061) Demobilization (15064) Narcotics control (16361)	Elections (15062) Human rights (15063) Land mine clearance (15066) Settlement (16330) Reconstruction relief (16340) Women in development (42010)
K	Free flow of information (15065) Statistical capacity building (16362) Agricultural research (31183) Technological research and development (32181) Culture and recreation (16350) Research and scientific institutions (16381)	Education sector (11xxx)

Source: Authors.

APPENDIX 5B. DIFFERENCES BETWEEN WORLD BANK (2001) AND THIS STUDY IN CLASSIFYING CRS SPENDING

The two classifications are broadly the same, with core spending (World Bank 2001) referring to IPGs (this study), and complementary spending (World Bank 2001) generally referring to NPGs (this study). Some differences also arise, because certain CRS items can, in principle, fall under more than one heading, for example, waste management relates to both environment and health. Specific differences are as follows:

- H related
  - Medical research (12182) in World Bank-core, but here as H-NPG
  - Waste management (14050) in World Bank-complementary, but here as E-IPG
  - Social services (16310) not in World Bank, but here as H-NPG
- E related
  - Energy education (23081), energy research (23082), environmental policy (41010), and environmental education and training (41081) in World Bank-complementary, but here as E-IPG

- Geothermal (23066), solar (23067), wind (23068), and biomass energy (23070) in World Bank-core, here as E-NPG
- Ocean power (23069), site preservation (41040), and flood prevention (41050) not in World Bank, here included as E-NPG
- Most agriculture-related items (31110, 31120, 31130, 31164, and 31165) not in World Bank, but here as E-NPG
- Low-cost housing (16220) and housing policy (16210) not in World Bank, but here as E-NPG
- G related
  - No subcategory governance in World Bank (except 15030, 15040, and 15050, which fall under the peace-core classification), but here some items as G-NPG
- P related
  - Settlement (16330), reconstruction relief (16340), and land mine clearance (15066) in World Bank-core, here as P-NPG
  - Emergency assistance (72010) in World Bank-core, but not included here
  - Narcotics control (16361) not in World Bank, here included as P-IPG
  - Elections (15062) and women in development (42010) not in World Bank, but here included as P-NPG
- K related
  - The education sector is included as K-NPG, but in World Bank educational research falls under core
  - Free flow of information (15065) is K-IPG, but is complementary in World Bank
  - Culture and recreation (16350) not in World Bank, but here as K-IPG.

NOTES

1. These estimates compare to about US$2 billion for core public goods and about US$8 billion for complementary public goods estimated in World Bank (2001).

2. Debt forgiveness as a share of total ODA rose from 3.3 percent during 1980–82 and 2.5 percent in 1985–87 to 15.5 percent in 1990–92, and then fell to 6.8 percent in 1996–98. Shares of debt forgiveness varied enormously by country and by year during the 1990s. Among the major bilateral donors the share in the late 1990s was 0.6 percent by Sweden, 2.1 percent by the United States, 4.5 percent by Japan, 7.1 percent by Denmark, 9.7 percent by the Netherlands, 14.6 percent by the United Kingdom, and 15.5 percent by France.

3. A recent resurgence has occurred in studies of whether aid contributes to economic growth. On the one hand, Burnside and Dollar (2000) argue that countries must have appropriate macroeconomic policies in place if aid is to be effective in promoting growth. On the other hand, Hansen and Tarp (2001) argue that aid tends to be effective even in countries with poor macroeconomic policies. In a review of the evidence, Morrissey (2001) argues that, on balance, aid does appear to contribute to growth. This debate on aid effectiveness is independent of global public good arguments for aid. However, if donors perceive aid as ineffective, they will be more likely to substitute financing of IPGs for other forms of aid.

4. The estimates suggest that the share of IPGs fell in 1985–87 relative to 1980–82, remained relatively flat thereafter, and then rose significantly in the 1990s. Our earlier finding of a secular increase in the share of aid devoted to public goods is consistent with these results in that in the 1980s, while the share of IPG to ODA rose, so did the ODA to GDP ratio, but the rise in the IPG to ODA ratio was slower than the rise in the ODA to GDP ratio in those years.

5. The results are not reported, but are available on request.

REFERENCES

Burnside, C., and D. Dollar. 2000. "Aid, Policies, and Growth." *American Economic Review* 90(4): 847–68.

Department for International Development. 2000. "Departmental Report 2000." London.

Hansen, H., and F. Tarp. 2001. "Aid and Growth Regressions." *Journal of Development Economics* 64(2): 547–70.

Hewitt, A., O. Morrissey, and D. W. te Velde. 2001. "Financing International Public Goods: Options for Resource Mobilisation." Report to the World Bank. Overseas Development Institute, London.

Kanbur, R., T. Sandler, with K. Morrison. 1999. *The Future of Development Assistance: Common Pools and International Public Goods.* Policy Essay no. 25. Washington, D.C.: Overseas Development Council.

Kaul, I., I. Grunberg, and M. Stern, eds. 1999. *Global Public Goods: International Cooperation in the 21st Century.* New York and Oxford: Oxford University Press.

Ministry of Foreign Affairs. 2000. *Homogene Groep Internationale Samenwerking 2001 (HGIS-nota).* The Hague.

Morrissey, O. 2001. "Does Aid Increase Growth?" *Progress in Development Studies* 1(1): 37–50.

Raffer, K. 1998. "ODA and Global Public Goods: A Trend Analysis of Past and Present Spending Patterns." Background paper. United Nations Development Programme, New York.

World Bank. 2001. "Effective Use of Development Finance for International Public Goods." *Global Development Finance.* Washington, D.C.

Chapter 6

REGIONAL PUBLIC GOODS IN OFFICIAL DEVELOPMENT ASSISTANCE

Marco Ferroni

One of the roles of official development assistance is to promote the delivery of public goods not provided by the market or by recipient governments in the absence of such assistance. This includes the provision of international public goods (IPGs), a challenge that has attracted growing attention in recent years. The case for IPGs, separable into global and regional public goods, arises from the collective action problems and strong externalities that are associated with such transnational challenges as financial contagion, the spread of communicable diseases, or the degradation of shared natural resources. Transnational development challenges—and the hard edges of globalization—are becoming more visible as countries become more interdependent and are more actively pursuing integration.

Controlling these challenges and harnessing the opportunities of globalization and integration require international cooperation. Sovereign nations must work together, and in the process must assert their sovereignty in new ways, that is, through contributions to mutually beneficial interdependence. However, collective action among sovereigns is difficult to achieve. Barrett (see chapter 3) explains why this is so, and why supplying truly global public goods is difficult. Different countries and their citizens value the benefits of public goods differently. This makes coordinating their production demanding (World Bank 2001a).

While some of the same problems arise in the provision of global public goods, the presumption is that coordination problems are likely to be less severe in supplying regional public goods. Experience shows that international organizations and official development assistance can help. This chapter looks at their role as catalysts and as sources and conduits of funding for regional public goods.

Regional public goods convey shared benefits to neighboring countries (countries within the region) and come in two forms: final and intermediate. Final goods are broad outcomes or manifestations of well-being, such as peace, the absence of extreme poverty, or a well-managed physical environment. They are the products of intermediate steps that themselves have some of the characteristics of public goods. Shared policy frameworks, regimes (such as regional integration schemes), institutions, and joint investments are examples of intermediate regional goods. Regional goods also arise when individual countries induce beneficial cross-border spillovers (regional "bads" arise in the case of undesirable spillovers). An epidemiological policy that improves domestic health while creating the externality of reduced transmission of pathogens and disease across borders is an example of an action generating a beneficial spillover.

Regional goods are often of a mixed nature, meaning that their benefits are not wholly public or shared by the countries in the region. Mixed goods bestow a combination of national and transnational benefits. Regional policies to pursue transnational benefits tend to be in short supply, because countries' first interest is their own national advantage. Countries acting on their own typically do not take into account the costs or effects of their actions on others. While governments often recognize that they could further their countries' national advantage by the right combination of national and regional policies, this by itself is usually not sufficient to overcome barriers to collective action.

In recent years, however, the demand for regional public goods has increased in the context of growing efforts at regional integration worldwide. Nations are undertaking these efforts with the aim of generating benefits that are shared by participating countries and cannot be obtained autonomously. The pursuit of commercial integration leads to, and indeed requires, cooperation in areas beyond trade, including infrastructure, finance, labor codes, public health, environmental standards, and other fields. Regional integration, therefore, provides a strong rationale for the study of regional public goods.

The objective of this chapter is threefold: (a) to review the demand, and the case, for regional public goods in the light of growing integration; (b) to report on the response of certain international organizations and the system of official development assistance to perceived growth in the demand for these goods; and (c) to analyze the challenges of financing regional public goods. The chapter is premised on the notion of complementarity between national and regional policies, the latter being seen as complements to, not substitutes for, the former.

International organizations are increasingly active in the area of regional public goods. Cook and Sachs (1999) deplore what they view as a low level of involvement in the provision of regional public goods on the part of official agencies. This chapter suggests, on the contrary, that official interest is strong and that operational involvement in the preparation of regional public goods (much of it researchable from the web sites of different institutions) is growing. The chapter shows that the Inter-American Development Bank (IDB), for example, has supported regional integration and cooperation aimed at producing regional and subregional public goods for many years. Thus an absence of awareness on the part of official agencies cannot explain today's undersupply of regional public goods. The undersupply is a consequence of collective action difficulties, countries' inability (politically or because of limited institutional capacity) to take the national measures that are needed to carry joint projects forward, and constrained multilateral instruments to catalyze action. As a consequence, multilateral institutions face disincentives to lend and governments to borrow for the provision of regional public goods. In addition, grant-based funding faces constraints.

The analysis of financing in this chapter focuses on activities and benefits that call for funding by the public sector. The chapter explores lending practices and the need for grants, and suggests some scope for innovation in the financing of regional public goods.

REGIONAL INTEGRATION AND THE DEMAND FOR REGIONAL PUBLIC GOODS

Currently, regional public goods cannot be discussed without reference to the worldwide trend toward regional integration. Regional and subregional commercial integration agreements have proliferated in the last 10 to 15 years. Most countries are now members of at least one such agreement (see the appendix to this chapter). Membership in regional agreements has grown for political reasons, as a substitute for the missing global round of trade negotiations, and perhaps because an imitation syndrome is at work (World Bank 2000b). Whatever the motivation, a historical trend toward regional groupings and cooperation is under way, complementing unilateral policies and multilateral cooperation.

The new regionalism was particularly evident in Latin America in the 1990s. Regional and subregional integration in the Americas has accompanied the process of broadly based structural reform that includes the state's withdrawal from direct economic activity, the promotion of private sector initiatives, and an opening to world markets (Devlin and Estevadeordal forthcoming; for further information on integration and trade in Latin America and the Caribbean see IDB 2000).

The proliferation of integration efforts is evidence that the demand for regional public goods is growing (CEIP 2001). The numerous agreements indicate an increasing willingness on the part of participating governments to engage in joint problem solving in selected areas of public policy. However, the road between articulating a demand for economic integration and actual, effective integration is arduous and long. To date trade blocs have yielded only limited integration among poor countries (box 6.1). They have worked better for more well-off countries; in cases where middle-income or transition countries were connected to Organisation for Economic Co-operation and Development

---

Box 6.1. Central American Integration

The case of Central America illustrates the difficulties of integration among poor countries. Achievements under the Central American Common Market, which was established in 1960 and modified in 1993, have not lived up to the expectations outlined in the political discourse over the years. The gains from trade integration in the form of widely spread scale, competition, and income effects have remained elusive. Integration and external competitiveness are held back by huge development problems in the constituent countries. By contrast, with the advent of peace in the region in the early 1990s, private actors began to promote the spontaneous integration of certain markets: banking and financial services, hotels, air transport, certain types of manufacturing, and retailing. As a result, intraregional trade and investment have grown considerably, driven by pragmatism rather than a particular political vision. To put this achievement on a firmer footing and set the stage for further expansion of investment and trade, governments must step in and provide rules of the game and an improved incentive framework to deepen integration. This includes the provision of better infrastructure, built and operated privately, where appropriate; the harmonization of policy in different fields; and the improvement of the determinants of competitiveness and economic performance through more effective national measures.

(OECD) economies through preferential arrangements; or, as in the case of the European Union, accession agreements.

The achievement of economies of scale and income convergence in regional agreements presupposes deeper integration than has been negotiated or achieved in most cases. The measures that are called for—reduced nontariff barriers; harmonized standards and rules, such as product safety rules; better cross-border infrastructure; improved customs procedures and border crossings; and other national measures that eliminate sources of trade friction and increase competition—are politically difficult to take. Regional agreements can assist by locking countries into reform commitments, accelerating—and increasing the credibility of—reciprocal measures to deepen integration. They can also help overcome negative neighborhood effects, that is, the pulling down of better performers by less well-performing neighbors.[1] However, the structural characteristics of poor neighboring economies may limit the economic gains that regional trade agreements can achieve and may cause the benefits to be distributed unevenly. Experience with integration agreements among poor countries suggests divergent economic outcomes and an absence of mechanisms to distribute gains equitably (World Bank 2000b). Examples of setbacks and conflict resulting from real or perceived asymmetry abound.

However, efforts at regional integration are here to stay. Technology, the evolution of the global economy, and global geopolitics after the end of the Cold War are conducive to international and regional cooperation. While some of the economic advantages pursued through regional commercial cooperation could be obtained through autonomous action and nonpreferential liberalization, other benefits, such as the regional stability expected from integration and the strengthening of a group's bargaining power relative to other trade blocs, cannot be realized without cooperation. For developing countries, regional integration affords opportunities for liberalization and reform in a more controlled and predictable setting than that encountered in a multilateral context. It also provides strategic impulses for development in areas beyond trade, leading to an induced demand for cooperation in different fields, for example, infrastructure, the harmonization of regulatory systems in finance, and product safety (Devlin and Ffrench-Davis 1998). By creating incentives and frameworks for cooperation, regional integration agreements contribute to problem solving and the rationalization of the use of shared resources in a range of domains, some of which are discussed in the next section.

STRENGTHENING NATIONAL DEVELOPMENT OUTCOMES THROUGH REGIONAL COOPERATION

Regional policies and programs can complement national development efforts in many areas: providing regional transport solutions and efficient patterns of energy trade, boosting national measures to overcome information barriers, stabilizing and regulating financial markets, containing endemic diseases, dealing with natural disasters, and preventing environmental degradation. In these and other policy domains, externalities and public goods arise, in principle, in three forms: beneficial cross-border spillovers, reduced harmful spillovers, and improved national outcomes—the ultimate test of the merits of international cooperation. The following paragraphs discuss the rationale for regional cooperation in different policy domains.

Transport

The coordination of transport infrastructure among neighboring countries is important for economic development. Surface transport is tied to geography, and location and geography play a role as determinants of development prospects (Gallup, Sachs, and Mellinger 1998). Transport costs are one mechanism through which location can affect incomes and economic growth. They are typically high for remote regions and landlocked developing countries. They need to be brought down for trade between producing and consuming regions in different countries to flourish.

   In the past, regional cooperation in the field of transport and other infrastructure has proven difficult to manage. Coastal countries may not consider it in their interest to improve and maintain roads or railroads for the benefit of landlocked neighbors (Cook and Sachs 1999). However, the climate for regional cooperation is improving in many parts of the developing world. While bilateral and regional conflicts continue to obviate trade and cross-border cooperation in some parts of the world, global political and economic trends in the post-Cold War era are fostering openness and integration. As a result, greater readiness to look at infrastructure from a transnational point of view is apparent worldwide. For example, the South American Regional Infrastructure Plan, unveiled at the summit of South American presidents in September 2000, identifies 12 key corridors linking the continent's countries. The plan addresses transportation, energy, and telecommunications needs along these corridors and provides for an integral and multisectoral approach to infrastructure development in coming years, with financing from the private sector, the IDB, the Corporación Andina de Fomento, and other institutions (IDB 2001). The recognition that regional integration cannot proceed without regional transport and infrastructure solutions is spreading in the developing world.

Energy

A growing number of developing countries is also attempting to improve energy efficiency by integrating the supply and distribution of energy. Making the supply of electricity more reliable and lowering unit costs requires competition and the attainment of economies of scale. This calls for small countries to integrate their power grids. Sparrow and Masters (1999) provide estimates of cost savings from electricity trade in southern Africa. Efforts at creating cross-border grids are under way in the Baltic countries, the Greater Mekong Subregion (ADB 2001), and elsewhere. In Central America work is under way to develop a regional power grid and create an integrated market for electricity serving a population of 34 million. Operating under a 1996 framework treaty signed by the six countries of the region, the initiative supports the establishment of an institutional and regulatory framework and funds investments to upgrade infrastructure for the transmission and distribution of power across borders. Framework agreements of this kind are a prerequisite for countries to begin to abandon costly self-sufficiency policies, but as always, the real challenge is implementation. In the absence of a strong overall integration platform, historical differences in regulatory structures and institutional weaknesses can make rationalizing the power sectors of neighboring countries a difficult proposition.

Data Transmission and Telecommunications

The infrastructure enabling telecommunications and data transmission is a core resource that countries need to compete in the global economy. While improving information infrastructure is largely a national issue, regional cooperation is needed to provide and regulate system backbones. Satellites and fiber optic cables tend to serve more than one country, and thus the transnational scale of competition among providers helps determine the price and quality of telecommunications and Internet services in individual countries (Cook and Sachs 1999).

The capacity of the system backbones serving developing countries deserves special attention. Backbone capacity serving developing countries is small compared with that at the disposal of OECD economies, a reality that has led to the emergence of a bandwidth divide as technology shifts from switched circuits to a packet-switching universe (DOT Force 2001). Based on International Telecommunication Union data as of late 2000, figure 6.1 shows that the bulk of Internet connectivity in gigabits per second is between the United States and Europe, and to a lesser extent, between the United States and the Asia-Pacific region. Africa has very thin lines reaching Europe and the United States, while the Latin American link to the United States is somewhat more robust, but frail with Europe. This situation forces local Internet providers in developing countries to purchase expensive international links to reach provider backbones in the North, raising the cost of access to users in poor countries. Cost increases from this source are additional to those that may arise from regulatory deficiencies and monopolistic market structures in these countries. Bandwidth considerations are thus an important aspect of the improved fiber loops that are needed to enhance connectivity (ITU 2001).

Financial Markets and Foreign Direct Investment

The possibility of cross-border financial contagion and, again, the desirability of bringing about economies of scale, are among the considerations in favor of regional approaches to regulating and stabilizing financial markets. Indeed, the absence of a regional focus is one reason why observers believe that financial sector reforms in Sub-Saharan Africa during the 1990s were disappointing (World Bank 2000a). The integration of the financial sectors of small, poorly-diversified economies can help lower both the costs and risks incurred by banks and financial service firms. Integration is often achieved through transborder consolidation of the industry. Policy measures promoting financial integration include harmonizing payments procedures, commercial and financial law, accounting standards, and prudential supervision. They also include appropriately endowed regional institutions to promote integration, help prevent crises through appropriate

Figure 6.1. International Internet Bandwidth

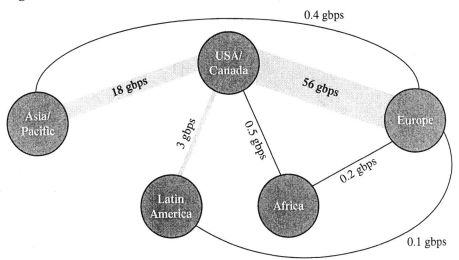

Gbps = Gigabits (1,000 Mb) per second.
Source: International Telecommunication Union data.

surveillance, and contribute to the stabilization of markets as a first line of defense, leaving the function of lender of last resort to global institutions such as the International Monetary Fund (Agosín 2000; Ocampo 2001).

In the competition for foreign direct investment, regional blocs can become a market brand and a means of recognition for potential investors. The bigger the regional market and the greater the locational advantages, the more attractive a bloc is likely to be to foreign investors (Devlin and Ffrench-Davis 1998). These forces are likely to favor integration agreements among better-off economies at the expense of groupings of poorer countries.

Public Health

Like financial contagion, communicable diseases, from AIDS to foot and mouth disease, call for transnational cooperation, because pathogens and financial disturbances do not stop at national borders. Human activity, including migration, travel, and trade, and natural agents, such as bacteria and viruses, insects, water-borne illnesses, and other forces, spread disease across borders. In this situation one country's negligence can easily nullify a neighboring country's epidemiological efforts. Coordinated international action can help.

Perhaps the best example of what a judicious combination of national and regional approaches can achieve is the River Blindness (onchocerciasis) Control Program in West Africa. The program (now extended to all oncho-endemic countries in Sub-Saharan Africa) has operated since 1974 through a coalition of African governments, local communities, international organizations, bilateral donors, the business sector, foundations, and nongovernmental organizations. It combines a regional focus with capacity building at the national and local levels, including the training of hundreds of epidemiologists, entomologists, and other specialists in national ministries of health and the signing on of tens of thousands of community health workers. River blindness, a debilitating disease transmitted by a fly, is now all but eradicated from the original program area, leading to enormous economic gains and improvements in the quality of life of the affected communities and individuals. The river blindness coalition has been held together by a strong sense of purpose shared by the participants, the right combination of leadership and submission on the part of individual contributors in accordance with their comparative advantages, a step-by-step approach following precisely defined and phased objectives, and the right amount of flexibility and compromise in execution (see http://www. worldbank.org/gper/ocp.htm).

Other Policy Concerns

This list of policy concerns in which regional cooperation can profitably complement national measures is incomplete. It could be extended, for example, to cover law enforcement, preservation or restoration of peace and security, management of natural resources and the environment, maintenance of cultural heritage, and research cooperation and knowledge sharing. Watershed management is particularly relevant in the realm of natural resources. On shared river systems, the use of water resources in one country can profoundly affect the quantity and quality of water available in downstream riparian countries. Diminishing water availability and water quality constrain economic development and can generate tensions, if not outright conflict. International law in the area of shared waters provides some guidance, but no universally accepted standards are available for the utilization and management of shared waters (John Briscoe, personal communication; see also the report on the 1998 International Round Table on Transboundary Water Management at http:// wbln0018.worldbank.org/essd.nsf). Riparian countries must search for cooperative solutions unique to their circumstances.

The International Consortium for Cooperation on the Nile is currently attempting to do this for the Nile River Basin. Like the River Blindness Control Program, the consortium, established in 1999, is a multiactor partnership of governments, donors, advocacy groups, the private sector, and international organizations. Its objective is to improve the management of the Nile River Basin, a resource shared by 10 countries from Egypt to Uganda, all of which suffer from water shortages and are affected by what from the collective viewpoint are suboptimal patterns of use of the Nile (see http://www.worldbank.org/ afr/nilebasin/).

Perspective

Examples such as the International Consortium for Cooperation on the Nile and other recent international initiatives and integration agreements indicate that cooperation among developing countries is on the rise. The recognition that regional policies and programs can generate dividends in terms of improved development outcomes at the national level appears to be spreading. This is a welcome development from the point of view of donors and aid recipients interested in development effectiveness. It does not mean that the challenges of collective action have become less formidable than they used to be. When it comes to individual initiatives, time-honored challenges such as political tensions, lack of trust, and high coordination costs persist, as do the difficulties of engineering equitable solutions acceptable to all parties.

Based on the considerations advanced in this and the previous sections, it is possible to formulate some requirements that should be fulfilled for regional cooperation to yield the full measure of benefits being pursued. First, regional cooperation must be extended far enough to make meaningful improvements possible. Eradicating the scourge of river blindness in West Africa took a generation, and appropriate national measures to keep the disease vector at bay will need to continue indefinitely. Eradication would not have been possible without persistence. Similarly, concluding a trade agreement is one thing, but persisting in the difficult effort of deepening integration, which may be needed to consolidate benefits over time, is quite another. Regional cooperation in the policy domains discussed earlier calls for long-term commitments on the part of those involved.

Second, participating countries must take the complementary national measures needed to enable them to contribute to, and absorb, the benefits of transnational cooperation. This is the hard part, more difficult than signing an international agreement and committing to the course of action that it implies. Regional cooperation consists of national measures taken in accordance with some agreed international plan. The absence of, or lags in, complementary national measures can bring the best collective action framework to naught.

Third, in the interest of sustainability, losers (or countries that gain less than others from cooperation in a given field) must be compensated to keep the coalition of actors and the pursuit of cooperative solutions alive.

Fourth, contracting parties should bind themselves with treaties or agreements that are self-enforcing where this is feasible, because of the absence of supranational authorities capable of exacting compliance. Barrett (chapter 3) shows that the requirement of self-enforcement reduces the number of feasible cooperative solutions.

These are demanding conditions, and they are seldom completely satisfied. Nevertheless, protagonists of regional initiatives ignore them at their risk.

REGIONAL PUBLIC GOODS IN OFFICIAL DEVELOPMENT ASSISTANCE

The system of official international assistance underwritten by bilateral aid agencies and multilateral institutions operates fundamentally on a country-by-country basis. At the same time it is responding to the call for regional and global public goods. Bilateral agencies and multilateral institutions bring different instruments to the task. Bilateral agencies promote regional or global endeavors indirectly by supporting activities coordinated by multilateral organizations. In financial terms, this support often takes the form of dedicated trust funds administered by multilateral agencies, mostly on a grant basis. Through their country programs, bilateral agencies can promote activities that help generate desirable cross-border externalities and can foster capacity in recipient countries that enables these countries to contribute to and take advantage of (or absorb) IPGs.

Because of their wide-ranging membership, multilateral agencies enjoy special legitimacy in promoting regional and global action. Such institutions, especially regional and subregional organizations, are stepping up their analysis of, and operational engagement in, regional activities. They promote transnational cooperation through a variety of functions: generating information, analyzing options and alternative courses of action, providing negotiation platforms and brokering agreements, supervising and enforcing standards and sanctions, and channeling financial resources.

This section reviews the evolving engagement of some multilateral entities and then presents evidence on the allocation of official flows to IPGs. Among the multilateral development banks, the IDB, the Asian Development Bank (ADB), and the World Bank are increasingly active in regional endeavors, the IDB and the ADB in their respective geographic areas of concentration and the World Bank in Sub-Saharan Africa, often in cooperation with the African Development Bank. The institutions intermediate grant funding from different sources to support regional integration and cooperation and experiment with regional loans to produce certain types of public goods and cross-border externalities. Through the credit enhancement instruments of their private sector arms they also support private investment in cross-border infrastructure. In general, they are engaged in the search for innovative ways to leverage their own resources for the purpose of promoting regional cooperation.

The Multilateral Development Banks and Regional Public Goods

The IDB, the ADB, and the World Bank illustrate the trend toward growing multilateral involvement in the production of regional public goods. The IDB has fostered regional cooperation since its inception, and during the 1990s expanded its involvement in the context of new and unprecedented interest in regional integration in Latin America and the Caribbean (Iglesias 2000). In addition to country-level programming, the bank programs operations at the regional and subregional levels and carries out research on regional integration. The Integration and Regional Programs Department serves as a focal point for regional issues, an institutional innovation not found in other multilateral development banks.

The IDB supports policy analysis and negotiation processes related to trade integration efforts at three levels: subregional (the Caribbean Community and Common Market, the Andean Community, the Central American Common Market, the Southern Common Market, and bilateral agreements), hemispheric (the proposed Free Trade Area of the Americas), and global in the context of negotiations at the World Trade Organization. In the financial area the IDB promotes the application of international standards that are needed both to preserve stability and promote financial integration. In regional infrastructure the IDB manages a portfolio of cross-border investments in transport infrastructure, border crossings, and energy, including gas pipelines. As an example, a privately owned and operated gas pipeline project received financing from the IDB's private sector window in 2000, together with support from a consortium of commercial banks, for a pipeline connecting northern Argentina and southern Brazil. New initiatives the IDB will support include the South American Regional Infrastructure Plan and the Plan Puebla-Panama, a recently unveiled regional development initiative covering southern Mexico and parts of Central America.

The IDB has long provided technical assistance on a regional basis. Regional technical cooperation supports research and knowledge management, training, and the creation and strengthening of institutions that foster regional integration. In 1999 the IDB created the Regional Policy Dialogue, a forum for policy discussion and strategic thinking in key areas pertaining to national development and Latin America's insertion into the global economy (see http://www.iadb.org/int/DRP/index.htm). The dialogue covers a variety of policy areas, including trade and integration, macroeconomic and financial policy, public management and transparency, poverty and social safety nets, education and human resources, and the environment and natural disaster management. It establishes networks of government officials proposed by the IDB's borrowing members, sponsors comparative studies that analyze experiences within and outside the region, maintains web-based resources, and organizes meetings and the dissemination of good practice. The IDB's regional policies and programs are financed by the bank's administrative budget, income from the Fund for Special Operations (the IDB's concessional window), donor trust funds, and limited lending.

The ADB supported regional policies and programs throughout the 1990s and has had a policy on regional cooperation since 1994. The bank's mission statement on regional cooperation states that the "ADB fosters economic growth and cooperation in the region, collectively and individually, and uses its resources for financing development in the region, giving priority to regional, subregional, and national projects" (http://www.adb.org/countries/cooperation.asp). Regional endeavors the ADB has supported include the promotion and institutionalization of economic cooperation in the Greater Mekong Subregion; the support of the Indonesia-Malaysia-Thailand growth triangle; the promotion of subregional cooperation in South Asia; and the fostering of trade cooperation among China, Kazakhstan, the Kyrgyz Republic, and Uzbekistan. The ADB supports regional technical cooperation and policy forums in areas ranging from the social sectors to competition policy, and from regional energy cooperation to telecommunications and health. Spending on regional technical cooperation is on the rise. The ADB also supports a growing number of regional road construction and rehabilitation projects financed by coordinated loans extended individually to the participating countries. More recently, the ADB's Regional Economic Monitoring Unit initiated regional economic monitoring to complement economic and financial surveillance at the national and global levels.

The World Bank tends to focus on global rather than regional cooperation, in keeping with its global nature and membership. The number of global partnerships supported by the World Bank has surged in recent years, with two-thirds of about 80 such partnerships being at most five years old. (The River Blindness Control Program is one of the oldest partnerships supported by the Bank.) As far as regional activities are concerned, the World Bank has concentrated on Sub-Saharan Africa, although all the World Bank's operational regions recognize the relevance of regional policies and programs. The World Bank has also sponsored regional activities in the Mekong Delta and the Caribbean. Together with the Commonwealth Secretariat, the Bank has recently supported work on the special development problems and external assistance needs of small states (Commonwealth Secretariat and World Bank 2000). The regional public good expected from this takes the form of improved policies by both donors and the countries concerned, leading to better development outcomes.

Regional cooperation and capacity building in Sub-Saharan Africa is undergoing a renaissance at the World Bank based on growing demand on the part of African governments, regional institutions, and donors for more systematic and coordinated approaches to regional integration (World Bank 2000a, 2001b). Subregional integration is accelerating in Sub-Saharan Africa (see the appendix to this chapter). As a result, the incentives to support regional cooperation are improving. Bank officials now believe that some past regional projects that failed were not conceived in the context of a coherent integration strategy. Today, the Bank sees the African subregional integration agreements of the 1970s and 1980s as having lacked the national support and cohesion needed to build sustainable regional partnerships. In today's new environment for regional cooperation, the World Bank is extending support to the preparation of a strategy for the Economic and Monetary Community of Central African States and for West Africa, following one for southern Africa and the Common Market for Eastern and Southern Africa that has existed since 1999. An active pipeline exists, much of it for regional technical cooperation. This is funded from the Bank's budget, the Institutional Development Fund (a grant program managed by the Bank), a grant from the African Development Fund (the concessional window of the African Development Bank), limited International Development Association grants, donor funds, the Bank's Project Preparation Facility, and funding from the Global Environment Facility for selected environmental concerns.

Growing Allocation of Official Flows to IPGs

The estimates now available regarding the allocation of official flows to IPGs attest to the growing involvement of official agencies in endeavors of transnational scope. Estimation of the share of official development spending devoted to IPGs is not straightforward, because the applicable data source—the OECD's Creditor Reporting System—does not permit information to be broken down according to whether spending categories are intended to generate multicountry or single country benefits (see chapter 5). The World Bank (2001a) has proposed separating development spending into core and complementary expenditures. Core expenditures finance regional and global programs undertaken with a multicountry interest in mind, for example, regional technical assistance to develop shared rules and standards that can help safeguard financial stability. Core expenditures also finance development activities that focus on individual countries, but whose benefits spill over to other countries.

The first type of core expenditure aims to create IPGs. The second type aims to create mixed goods as defined earlier. Complementary expenditures finance activities that enable developing countries to take advantage of the IPGs and cross-border externalities emerging from core activities.

Ignoring spending on physical infrastructure, much of which is now financed privately, official spending on core and complementary activities in four areas (health, the environment, knowledge enhancement, and peacekeeping and security) amounted to about US$15 billion per year in the second half of the 1990s, up sharply from the 1970s and 1980s (World Bank 2001a). This includes trust funds, country-based bilateral spending, and multilateral concessional and nonconcessional lending.

Te Velde, Morrissey, and Hewitt (chapter 5) offer more detailed analysis of the allocation of aid to IPGs. Neither their study nor the World Bank's distinguish empirically between regional and global public goods because of data limitations.

Further analysis would not only have to make that distinction, but would also have to address two other issues. The first is how the donor community prioritizes the IPGs that it wishes to support. Priorities always emerge through a combination of analysis and political processes, but setting priorities for IPGs is both less well established than country programming and more complicated, in part because it involves a larger number of actors than the donor-recipient country relationship at work in country programming exercises. The second is whether spending on IPGs is additional to spending on country programs (see chapter 5, whose authors doubt the existence of financial additionality). Compared with the alternative of solely country-focused assistance, the judicious combination of support to national and transnational problem solving is expected to yield additionality in terms of development impact. By the analysis advanced in this chapter, this is the rationale for going transnational. The nature and size of this additionality in specific instances deserves to be investigated more systematically.

Further increases in official spending on IPGs would have to be justified by evidence regarding their development impact on the ground. However, while such evidence can probably be produced, resource constraints arising from disincentives to lending for IPGs and from the limited availability of grant-based funds will likely cap the growth of spending on IPGs in the future as they have in the past.

THE FINANCING OF REGIONAL PUBLIC GOODS

Official finance to support the production and absorption of regional public goods comes in the form of loans and grants. Loans are the more abundant resource, and should therefore be used before grants whenever possible. They are also preferable because of their tendency to strengthen borrower ownership of the activity in question and their educational role in promoting a credit culture in recipient countries where this may be needed. However, loans may not work for all aspects of IPGs. The choice between loans and grants is informed by the distinction between core and complementary activities pertaining to the production and absorption of international and regional public goods.

We defined core activities as activities to create IPGs and as measures to create mixed goods. The selection of the right funding instrument is relatively straightforward in the case of the first kind of core activities and in the case of complementary activities. It is more complicated in the case of mixed goods.

Core activities of the first kind tend to call for grant-based funding, whereas complementary activities can be financed using loans. Borrowers have an incentive to take out loans for complementary activities that support absorption, because all the associated benefits accrue to them and (at least in terms of first-order effects) do not spill over to others. The loans would be concessional or nonconcessional, depending on the status of the borrower as an International Development Association or an International Bank for Reconstruction and Development country, to use World Bank parlance.

Grants

The case for grants for core activities arises, because these activities generate benefits that invite free-riding. Nonpaying parties cannot be excluded from the benefits being created. Hence partnerships such as the Consultative Group on International Agricultural Research, a global program, or the more recently established Regional Fund for Agricultural Technology in Latin America and the Caribbean are funded on a grant basis (the latter is funded by an endowment provided by its regional member countries and institutions). Grant-based global and regional programs coordinated by the different multilateral development banks are similar in terms of their basic orientation and objectives. They promote research, knowledge management, emergency preparedness, training and institution building, and policy discussions among bank member countries to create awareness and possibly consensus regarding ways to address certain problems. The IDB's Regional Policy Dialogue is funded on a grant basis, and it is difficult to see how this could be otherwise. Another example of a grant program sponsored by the IDB is the Inter-American Institute for Social Development, set up to provide strategic capabilities to the social area management teams of the governments of Latin America and the Caribbean (see http://www.iadb.org/indes).

However, while grants are necessary for some kinds of programs, their allocation, governance, and management can be challenging. Because they are free, an element of moral hazard may be associated with grants. The demand for grants is unlimited, by definition. Donors, international organizations, and issue-focused civil society groups formulate numerous calls for activities intended to produce international and regional public goods. In this situation, having transparent and participatory methods for setting priorities is extremely important, and the provenance of grant funding is important in this context. The multilateral banks must strike the right balance between grants funded from the administrative budget (controlled by all members in accordance with their voting rights) and funds made available by individual donors.

The multilateral banks and their shareholders must also be transparent with respect to the issue of burden sharing. The allocation of income derived from lending operations to finance IPGs represents a cost to the banks' larger borrowers (the borrowers that do not have access to concessional resources), because it leads to increased loan charges to meet income targets. In the eyes of the nonborrowers: "Because the loans are subsidized by their guarantee of the [banks'] liabilities, the effect on the cost of borrowing is not a measure of the cost of financing regional or global public goods" (CEIP 2001, p. 31).

Other issues that must be addressed include the leverage that grant funds should induce, for example, via cost sharing among the beneficiaries; the relationship between the grantor and grantees, which should be arms-length; and the assurance that innovation is being fostered under grant programs. Further aspects include the existence of an exit strategy, clarity with respect to subsidiarity or the subordination of grants to lending, and grantor awareness that an entitlement mentality could spread among grantees, which could tie up funds in the long-term that might more appropriately go to new endeavors. Therefore, while the call for grant funding for the production of IPGs is justified, the free nature of this financial resource (free from the recipients' point of view) should not detract from the need for ambitious, goal-oriented standards of deployment and rigorous monitoring and evaluation.

However, grant programs are often not evaluated, except in the case of large and long-standing programs that are known to have produced important international and regional public goods, for example, the River Blindness Control Program. Unpublished evaluation reports produced by some of the multilateral banks indicate that many small grant programs and regional technical cooperation activities do not have well-defined monitoring systems and are not systematically evaluated. The developmental impact of some long-standing grant programs administered by international agencies is not well documented. Thus calls for grant funding to support the provision of international and regional public goods should go hand in hand with calls for adequate monitoring and evaluation.

Loans

When it comes to financing mixed goods, borrowers hold loans in low esteem. They are reluctant to take on loan charges when they cannot capture most of the benefits expected from the investment financed by the loan. Countries' reluctance to borrow is likely to grow with the magnitude of the expected cross-border externality relative to national gain. Eradicating (or greatly lowering the prevalence of) tuberculosis in an endemic country yields a higher gain to that country than to others as long as much of the world is still prone to this disease, but eradicating the remaining pockets of poliomyelitis yields a larger gain to the rest of the world than to the few developing countries in which the disease occurs sporadically. Similarly, preserving forests and biodiversity may produce a larger gain for the rest of the world than for individual forest-rich lands. Should these countries be the only ones to pay for vestigial disease eradication campaigns or the preservation of natural resources? Or should they be compensated by those benefiting from the externalities?

Compensation brings up the issue of differential pricing for services that generate cross-border benefits. Differential pricing is on the table in discussions spearheaded by the Group of Seven on the products and governance of the multilateral banks. The discussion has not focused explicitly on financing global and regional public goods, but it could be extended to this topic. In between grants and regularly priced nonconcessional loans at near-market rates, there is room for a gradient of incentives in the form of differentially priced concessional loans that would compensate borrowers for precious externalities originating from their territory.

The World Bank (2001a) argues that differential pricing, that is, lower interest charges for some investment loans, needs to be judged on efficiency grounds, because it does not expand the envelope of resources. Differential pricing would, in theory, permit fine-tuning of subsidies for different kinds of IPGs, but it could also be difficult to administer, with administration likely becoming a politically charged exercise. Multilateral financial institutions have basically offered two kinds of loans—concessional and nonconcessional—for many years, with borrowers' eligibility for each type being a function of their income and (implicitly) creditworthiness. The addition of an IPG criterion, while worthwhile, could complicate matters considerably. Borrowing and nonborrowing shareholders would have to engage in negotiations to agree about which IPGs to pursue, and nonborrowing shareholders would have to admit the principle of loan subsidies for the better-off developing countries that do not qualify for concessional loans.

In the absence of differential pricing, loans will need to be combined with grant funding in appropriate combinations to foster the production of mixed goods. This is already being done in the form of hybrid financial products combining concessional or nonconcessional lending and grant-based co-financing from bilateral donors. The Global Environment Facility is a source of grant-based co-financing for operations that address global environmental issues, but the facility is small in relation to needs, as are the resources that bilateral donors have been able to make available. No dedicated international funds for priorities other than the global environment are available (though the international community has recently agreed to establish a global AIDS fund). Funds for regional priorities are even scarcer. In addition, grant funding tends to go largely to the poorest countries, which is appropriate from the point of view of fostering development within national confines, but may be inappropriate if one seeks to maximize cross-border externalities in key areas of transnational public policy.

In principle, a solution exists to the problem of financing such endeavors as cross-border infrastructure and campaigns to combat contagious disease: multicountry loans taken out jointly by the members of a spillover community or by countries that otherwise stand to benefit from coordinated action. In practice, however, such loans are difficult to manage. The difficulty lies in figuring out and obtaining agreement on who should pay what share of the cost of borrowing. This makes it difficult for official financial institutions to employ their basic financial instrument, a government-guaranteed loan, to support the creation of international and regional public goods.

World Bank Experience with Multicountry Loans

The portfolio of multicountry or regional loans held by multilateral development banks is small. The World Bank, for example, has extended less than 50 regional loans in its entire history. Table 6.1 shows 44 multicountry projects by region, sector, and when they were approved. Of these operations, 27 were located in Sub-Saharan Africa, 9 in the Caribbean, 4 in Latin America, 2 in Europe and Central Asia, and 1 each in the Middle East and North Africa and South Asia. The concentration in Africa and the Caribbean may be explained by the particularly small size of national economies in these regions, prompting a search for economies of scale through regional cooperation (see Ferroni and Hassberger 2000).

Every loan shown in the table represents a world of challenges and arrangements, making meaningful comparisons difficult. Nevertheless, these loans essentially employed variations of three lending modalities: single country loans with a binational (or regional) objective embedded in binational (or regional) agreements, loans to multinational entities such as subregional development banks and special purpose companies established for the project, and individual coordinated loans to participating sovereign borrowers.

The Indus River project is perhaps the most famous example of the first kind of loan arrangement in the history of multilateral development banking. In September 1960, India, Pakistan, and the World Bank signed the Indus Water Treaty, which governs the use of the waters of the Indus River system. Signature of the treaty marked the end of a long-standing dispute between India and Pakistan. Under the treaty the Indus Basin Development Fund of almost US$900 million (subsequently augmented by a further US$300 million) was established to finance the construction of irrigation and other works in Pakistan that were needed to enable the country to use and develop its share of the Indus River system. Contributions from Western governments and World Bank "single-country" loans to Pakistan financed the fund.

The second type of regional loans with which the World Bank experimented was fraught with difficulty. In the 1970s it included a number of finance and

Table 6.1. World Bank Regional Projects by Sectors and Decades, 1960s–2000s

Sector	Africa	Caribbean	Latin America	Europe and Central Asia	Middle East and North Africa	South Asia	Total	1960s	1970s	1980s	1990s	2000s
Finance	7	5	0	0	0	0	12	0	3	4	3	2
Transportation	6	0	0	1	1	0	8	0	4	2	0	2
Electric power	3	0	2	0	0	0	5	0	0	3	2	0
Oil and gas	2	0	2	0	0	0	4	1	0	1	1	1
Telecommunications	3	1	0	0	0	0	4	1	2	0	1	0
Environment	1	1	0	1	0	0	3	0	0	0	2	1
Agriculture	1	0	0	0	0	1	2	1	1	0	0	0
Industry	2	0	0	0	0	0	2	0	1	1	0	0
Water supply	1	0	0	0	0	0	1	0	0	0	1	0
Education	0	1	0	0	0	0	1	0	0	1	0	0
Health	1	0	0	0	0	0	1	0	0	0	0	1
Public sector management	0	1	0	0	0	0	1	0	0	0	1	0
Total	27	9	4	2	1	1	44	3	11	12	11	7

Source: Ferroni and Hassberger (2000).

infrastructure loans extended to subregional entities. For example, several World Bank loans to the Banque Ouest Africaine de Développement sought to strengthen the borrowing institution's development role and contribution to regional integration. The loans helped finance feasibility and engineering studies for regional infrastructure projects, as well as some of these projects themselves. According to an internal project completion report, the World Bank deemed the projects successful at strengthening the recipient intermediary, but encountered significant problems at the subproject level because of difficulties in obtaining government commitment for regional projects. This caused the authors of the report to conclude that regional and subregional projects, involving more than one country, are scarce and difficult to realize. Similar conclusions emerged from regional infrastructure projects in East Africa. Six different loans extended by the World Bank to the Caribbean Development Bank between 1976 and 1994 also faced problems, compounded by difficulties related to the World Bank's guarantee requirement, which called for sovereign subloan guarantees from each Caribbean Development Bank borrowing country to which loan proceeds were on-lent. The exasperated authors of a project performance audit report at the time indicated that the amount of administrative work required to provide these guarantees cannot be exaggerated.

Multinational projects are much more complex and risky than national ones. Synchronizing project phases in different countries can be difficult. In addition, participating countries face different political and economic circumstances and cycles, and may proceed at different rhythms because of differences in institutional capacity. This can be a source of tension if one party is holding the others back. These and other issues can translate into high transaction costs that can deter well-meaning potential participants and international organizations.

The third type of regional program lending, a set of individual coordinated loans to sovereign borrowers, has not been tried much, but would appear to be promising as a way to overcome disincentives to borrowing, and thus to regional cooperation. The new Multicountry HIV/AIDS Program for Sub-Saharan Africa supported by the World Bank seeks to channel resources to countries and regional organizations to strengthen and expand disease prevention and care measures under a joint policy approach. Individual country operations are meant to proceed according to local rhythms reflecting implementation capacity under national action plans, but following a regional approach. There would seem to be considerable scope for innovation along these lines. A joint approach would enhance impact and eliminate free-riding and disincentives to take out loans, and would thereby make more resources available to address urgent issues of transnational scope. The resources certainly exist; multilateral development banks have been lending less in recent years than they could have. However, the approach calls for a strong advocacy and collective action-enhancing role by these institutions. The challenge of obtaining agreement on a common platform of action can be daunting.

The wider deployment of the described approach to coordinated lending would make it necessary for the institutions to overcome internal organizational setups that militate against communication across divisions and departments responsible for different countries belonging to the same spillover group. More generally, the culture of approaching problems from a regional point of view would have to be further strengthened, and the institutions' administrative budgets would have to accommodate what must be assumed to be heavy transaction costs of building partnerships and coalitions for joint action financed on the basis of loans. Coordinated loans extended under a common policy framework, but permitting as much national autonomy in program execution as possible without jeopardizing the common framework, would appear to offer the best scope for purposeful, loan financed, regional cooperation.

CONCLUSION

The worldwide trend toward regional integration creates incentives for cooperation in a range of policy domains beyond international trade. Multilateral and bilateral institutions known for their country focus are supportive of this trend and are increasingly engaged in regional policies and programs. Their aim is to realize the development dividends at the national level that can be expected from investing in core and complementary activities related to international and regional public goods. The chapter analyzes how regional public goods are being financed through lending and nonlending operations and clarifies the circumstances under which lending is possible and when grant funding is in order. There is some scope for innovation in regional lending, with the instrument of choice being a program of coordinated loans offered to and taken out by countries that belong to a given spillover community. Brokering arrangements of this kind are challenging, but the rewards could be substantial in an era in which growing international interdependence calls for an increased supply of regional public goods.

APPENDIX. MEMBERSHIP OF SELECTED MAJOR REGIONAL INTEGRATION AGREEMENTS AND YEAR OF FORMATION

INDUSTRIAL AND DEVELOPING ECONOMIES

European Union (EU): formerly European Economic Community (EEC) and European Community (EC), **1957**: Belgium, France, Germany, Italy, Luxembourg, Netherlands; **1973**: Denmark, Ireland, United Kingdom; **1981**: Greece; **1986**: Portugal, Spain; **1995**: Austria, Finland, Sweden.

European Economic Area (EEA): **1994**: EU, Iceland, Liechtenstein, Norway.

Euro-Mediterranean Economic Area (Euro-Maghreb): bilateral agreements, **1995**: EU, Tunisia; **1996**: EU and Morocco.

EU bilateral agreements with Eastern Europe: **1994**: EC, Hungary, Poland; **1995**: EC, Bulgaria, Romania, Estonia, Latvia, Lithuania, Czech Republic, Slovak Republic, Republic of Slovenia.

Canada-US Free Trade Area (CUFTA): **1988**: Canada, United States.

North American Free Trade Area (NAFTA): **1994**: Canada, Mexico, United States.

Asia Pacific Economic Cooperation (APEC): **1989**: Australia, Brunei Darussalam, Canada, Indonesia, Japan, Republic of Korea, Malaysia, New Zealand, the Philippines, Singapore, Thailand, United States; **1991**: People's Republic of China, Taiwan (China), Hong Kong (China); **1993**: Mexico, Papua New Guinea; **1994**: Chile; **1998**: Peru, Russia, Vietnam.

LATIN AMERICA AND THE CARIBBEAN

Andean Pact: **1969**: revived in 1991, Bolivia, Colombia, Ecuador, Peru, Venezuela.

Central American Common Market (CACM): **1960**: revived in 1993, El Salvador, Guatemala, Honduras, Nicaragua; **1962**: Costa Rica.

Southern Common Market, Mercado Común del Sur (MERCOSUR): 1991: Argentina, Brazil, Paraguay, Uruguay.

Group of Three (G3): 1995: Colombia, Mexico, Venezuela.

Latin American Integration Association (LAIA): formerly Latin American Free Trade Area (LAFTA), **1960**: revived 1980, Argentina, Bolivia, Brazil, Chile, Colombia, Ecuador, Mexico, Paraguay, Peru, Uruguay, Venezuela.

Caribbean Community and Common Market (CARICOM): 1973: Antigua and Barbuda, Barbados, Jamaica, St. Kitts and Nevis, Trinidad and Tobago; **1974**: Belize, Dominica, Grenada, Montserrat, St. Lucia, St. Vincent and the Grenadines; **1983**: The Bahamas (part of the Caribbean Community but not of the Common Market).

AFRICA

Cross-Border Initiative (CBI): 1992: Burundi, Comoros, Kenya, Madagascar, Malawi, Mauritius, Namibia, Rwanda, Seychelles, Swaziland, Tanzania, Uganda, Zambia, Zimbabwe.

East African Cooperation (EAC): 1967: formerly East African Community (EAC), broke up in 1977 and recently revived, Kenya, Tanzania, Uganda.

Economic and Monetary Community of Central Africa (CEMAC): 1994: formerly Union Douanière et Economique de l'Afrique Centrale (UDEAC), **1966**: Cameroon, Central African Republic, Chad, Congo, Gabon; **1989**: Equatorial Guinea.

Economic Community of West African States (ECOWAS): 1975: Benin, Burkina Faso, Cape Verde, Côte d'Ivoire, The Gambia, Ghana, Guinea, Guinea-Bissau, Liberia, Mali, Mauritania, Niger, Nigeria, Senegal, Sierra Leone, Togo.

Common Market for Eastern and Southern Africa (COMESA): 1993: Angola, Burundi, Comoros, Djibouti, Egypt, Ethiopia, Kenya, Lesotho, Malawi, Mauritius, Mozambique, Rwanda, Somalia, Sudan, Swaziland, Tanzania, Uganda, Zambia, Zimbabwe.

Indian Ocean Commission (IOC): 1984: Comoros, Madagascar, Mauritius, Seychelles.

Southern African Development Community (SADC): 1980: formerly known as the Southern African Development Coordination Conference (SASCC), Angola, Botswana, Lesotho, Malawi, Mozambique, Swaziland, Tanzania, Zambia, Zimbabwe; **1990**: Namibia; **1994**: South Africa; **1995**: Mauritius; **1998**: Democratic Republic of the Congo, Seychelles.

Economic Community of West Africa (CEAO): 1973: revived in 1994 as UEMOA, Benin, Burkino Faso, Côte d'Ivoire, Mali, Mauritania, Niger, Senegal.

West African Economic and Monetary Union (UEMOA or WAEMU): 1994: Benin, Burkina Faso, Côte d'Ivoire, Mali, Niger, Senegal, Togo; **1997**: Guinea-Bissau.

Southern African Customs Union (SACU): 1910: Botswana, Lesotho, Namibia, South Africa, Swaziland.

Economic Community of the Countries of the Great Lakes (CEPGL): 1976: Burundi, Rwanda, Democratic Republic of the Congo.

MIDDLE EAST AND ASIA

Association of South-East Asian Nations (ASEAN): 1967: ASEAN Free Trade Area (AFTA) was created in 1992, Indonesia, Malaysia, the Philippines, Singapore, Thailand; **1984**: Brunei Darussalam; **1995**: Vietnam; **1997**: Myanmar, Lao People's Democratic Republic; **1999**: Cambodia.

Gulf Cooperation Council (GCC): 1981: Bahrain, Kuwait, Oman, Qatar, Saudi Arabia, the United Arab Emirates.

South Asian Association for Regional Cooperation (SAARC): 1985: Bangladesh, Bhutan, India, Maldives, Nepal, Pakistan, Sri Lanka.

Source: World Bank (2000b).

NOTE

1. Easterly and Levine (1997) estimate that neighborhood effects may shave economic growth in Sub-Saharan Africa by up to 1 percentage point. The World Bank (2000a) notes that sometimes neighborhood effects may be merely reputational, a kind of "guilt by association mortgage" hanging over better performing and more reform-minded members of a community.

REFERENCES

The word processed describes informally reproduced works that may not be commonly available through libraries.

ADB (Asian Development Bank). 2001. *Annual Report 2000.* Manila.

Agosín, M. R. 2000. "Fortaleciendo la institucionalidad financiera en Latinoamérica." Temas de Coyuntura series. Economic Commission for Latin America and the Caribbean, Santiago.

CEIP (Carnegie Endowment for International Peace). 2001. "The Role of the Multilateral Development Banks in Emerging Market Economies: New Policies for a Changing Global Environment." Report of the Commission on the Role of the Multilateral Development Banks in Emerging Markets. Washington, D.C.

Commonwealth Secretariat and World Bank. 2000. "Small States: Meeting Challenges in the Global Economy." Report of the Commonwealth Secretariat and World Bank Joint Task Force on Small States. Washington, D.C. Processed.

Cook, L., and J. Sachs. 1999. "Regional Public Goods in International Assistance." In I. Kaul, I. Grunberg, and M. Stern, eds., *Global Public Goods: International Cooperation in the 21st Century.* New York and Oxford: Oxford University Press.

Devlin, R., and R. Ffrench-Davis. 1998. "Towards an Evaluation of Regional Integration in Latin America in the 1990s." Working Paper no. 2. Inter-American Development Bank and Institute for the Integration of Latin America and the Caribbean. Washington, D.C.

Devlin, R. and A. Estevadeordal. Forthcoming. "What's New in the New Regionalism in the Americas?" In V. B. Thomas, ed., *Regional Integration in Latin America and the Caribbean: The Political Economy of Open Regionalism.* London: Institute of Latin American Studies.

DOT Force (Digital Opportunities Task Force). 2001. "Digital Opportunities for All: Meeting the Challenge." Draft report. Plenary Meeting, April 23–24, Siena, Italy.

Easterly, W., and R. Levine. 1997. "Africa's Growth Tragedy: Policies and Ethnic Divisions." *Quarterly Journal of Economics* 112 (November): 1203–50.

Ferroni, M., and A. Hassberger. 2000. "Regional Public Goods and the World Bank's Experience with Regional Loans." World Bank, Washington, D.C. Processed.

Gallup, J. L., J. Sachs, and A. D. Mellinger. 1998. "Geography and Economic Development." Working Paper no. W6849. National Bureau for Economic Research, Cambridge, Massachusetts.

IDB (Inter-American Development Bank). 2000. "Integration and Trade in the Americas." Periodic Note. Washington, D.C.

———. 2001. "Summit of the Americas—Strategic Programs: The Agenda of the IDB." Quebec.

Iglesias, E. 2000. "Doce lecciones de cinco décadas de integración regional en América Latina y el Caribe." Presentation given at the Institute for the Integration of Latin America and the Caribbean, Buenos Aires, November 27. Inter-American Development Bank, Integration and Regional Programs Department. Washington, D.C.

ITU (International Telecommunication Union). 2001. "Numbering Cyberspace: Recent Trends in the Internet World." ITU Telecommunication Indicators Update January-February-March 2001. Geneva.

Ocampo, J. A. 2001. "Recasting the International Financial Agenda." In J. Eatwell and L. Taylor, eds., *External Liberalization, Economic Performance, and Social Policy.* New York: Oxford University Press.

Sparrow, F. T., and W. A. Masters. 1999. "Modeling Electricity Trade in Southern Africa 1999–2000." Purdue University, West Lafayette, Indiana.

World Bank. 2000a. *Can Africa Claim the 21st Century?* Washington, D.C.

———. 2000b. *Trade Blocs.* Washington, D.C.

———. 2001a. *Global Development Finance: Building Coalitions for Effective Development Finance.* Washington, D.C.

———. 2001b. "Toward a Systematic Approach to Regional Integration." Africa Region. World Bank, Washington, D.C. Processed.

INDEX

Advanced Research Projects Agency
  (Department of Defense), 22
Africa
    energy industry in, 163
    regional activities in, 171–172
    regional integration agreements
      in, 183–184
African Development Bank, 169
African Virtual University, 122
Aggregation technology
    best shot, 96, 99–100
    summation, 95–97
    weakest link, 96, 98–99
    weighted sum, 96, 100–101
Agreement Concerning the Estab-
  lishing of Global Technical Regu-
  lations for Wheeled Vehicles, 62
Aid allocation
    conclusions regarding, 151–152
    CRS spending classifications
      and, 154–155
    in developing countries as share
      of donor GDP, 137–140
    for IPGs, 140–144
    for national and international
      public goods, 120–124,
      153–154

The Netherlands case study on,
      148–151
    overview of, 119–120
    by sector, 124–125, 132–137
    share allocated to public goods,
      125–132
    United Kingdom case study on,
      145–147, 151
Albendazole, 45
American Economic Association, 85
American Political Science Associa-
  tion, 85
Asia, 184
Asian Development Bank (ADB),
  169, 171
Automobile emissions, 61–62

Baland, J.-M., 51
Banque Ouest Africaine de
    Développement, 180
Barrett, Scott, 8, 9, 11, 12, 19, 53
Benefit principle, 83–84
Best shot goods, 9, 10, 22
Best shot technology, 96, 99–100
Boyer, J. G., 13
British Aid Statistics, 145